ETHICS OF SOCIALLY DISRUPTIVE TECHNOLOGIES

Ethics of Socially Disruptive Technologies

An Introduction

Edited by
Ibo van de Poel, Lily Frank, Julia Hermann,
Jeroen Hopster, Dominic Lenzi, Sven
Nyholm, Behnam Taebi, and Elena Ziliotti

OpenBook
Publishers

Contents

List of abbreviations

AI: Artificial Intelligence

AIBO: Artificial Intelligence Robot; in Japanese aibō means "pal" or "partner"

BECCS: Bioenergy with Carbon Capture and Storage

CCS: Carbon Capture and Storage

CDR: Carbon Dioxide Removal

ChatGPT: Chat Generative Pre-training Transformer

CRISPR-cas9: CRISPR-associated protein 9, where CRISP stands for Clustered Regularly Interspaced Short Palindromic Repeats

DACCS: Direct Air Capture with Carbon Storage

ESDiT: Ethics of Socially Disruptive Technologies (research program)

EUFI: Unified Extensible Firmware Interface

EW: Enhanced Weathering

GBAM: Ground-based Albedo Modification

GHG: Greenhouse Gasses

LaMDA: Language Model for Dialogue Applications

LGBTQ+ : Lesbian, Gay, Bisexual, Transgender, Queer and many other terms (such as non-binary and pansexual)

MCB: Marine Cloud Brightening

IAU: International Astronomical Union

IPBES:	Intergovernmental Science-Policy Platform on Biodiversity and Ecosystem Services
IPCC:	Intergovernmental Panel on Climate Change
IVF:	In Vitro Fertilization
NGO:	Non-Governmental Organization
NH:	New Hampshire
OF:	Ocean Fertilization
SAI:	Solar Aerosol Injection
SRM:	Solar Radiation Management
STEM:	Science, Technology, Engineering and Mathematics
VSD:	Value Sensitive Design
WEIRD:	Western, Educated, Industrialized, Rich, and Democratic

Contributor Biographies

Dina Babushkina is an Assistant Professor in philosophy of technology and society at the University of Twente. She researches the ways AI (and social robotics) affect, change, and disrupt interpersonal relationships, personhood and human lived experiences, with special attention to human cognitive practices and decision making. ORCID: 0000-0003-4899-8319

Philip Brey is a Professor in philosophy and ethics of technology at the University of Twente and leader of the ESDiT programme. His research is in general ethics of technology, in which he investigates new approaches for ethical assessment, guidance and design of emerging technologies, and in ethics of digital technologies, with a focus on AI, robotics, internet, virtual reality and the metaverse. ORCID: 0000-0002-4789-4588

Lorina Buhr is a Postdoctoral Researcher at Utrecht University. Her research examines conceptual, ontological and normative aspects of finitude and irreversibility in nature, using the examples of extinction and technologies for de-extinction. ORCID: 0000-0002-0718-6026

Stefan Buijsman is an Assistant Professor at Delft University of Technology and works on explainable AI and related epistemic challenges to responsible AI. ORCID: 0000-0002-0004-0681

Kristy Claassen is a PhD candidate at the University of Twente. Her research focuses on intercultural philosophy, Ubuntu and artificial intelligence. ORCID: 0000-0001-5162-2529

Michael T. Dale is an Assistant Professor of philosophy at Hampden-Sydney College. He is currently interested in exploring to what extent empirical findings can have implications for the ethics of artificial intelligence and social robotics. ORCID: 0000-0001-7827-5248

Matthew J. Dennis is an Assistant Professor in ethics of technology at Eindhoven University of Technology. His research investigates how technology can be designed to promote autonomy, fairness, and well-being. ORCID: 0000-0002-4212-6862

Lily Eva Frank is an Assistant Professor of philosophy and ethics at Eindhoven University of Technology where she works on technologies of the body and ways in which they can be ethically and socially disruptive. ORCID: 0000-0001-8659-2390

Cindy Friedman is a PhD candidate at the Ethics Institute, Utrecht University. Her research focuses on the ethics of social robots, with a particular focus on humanoid robots, and the ethics of human-robot interaction. ORCID: 0000-0002-4901-9680

Alessio Gerola is a PhD candidate in the Philosophy Group of Wageningen University. He explores the philosophical and ethical impacts of biomimetic design, the intentional imitation of nature for technological innovation. ORCID: 0000-0003-4417-9367

Arthur Gwagwa is a PhD candidate at the Ethics Institute at Utrecht University. His research focuses on anti-domination approaches in new frontier technological and data relationships between the Global North and China and the Global South. ORCID: 0000-0001-9287-3025

Julia Hermann is an Assistant Professor of philosophy and ethics at the University of Twente where she works on ectogestative technology, care robots, technomoral change and progress, and new methodologies in the ethics of technology. ORCID: 0000-0001-9990-4736

Ben Hofbauer is a PhD candidate at Delft University of Technology, in the faculty for Technology, Policy & Management. His work focuses on the ethical implications of the research on, and potential deployment of solar climate engineering technologies. ORCID: 0000-0003-4839-5315

Jeroen Hopster is an Assistant Professor of ethics at Utrecht University. His research centers on climate ethics and on investigating the nature of socially disruptive technologies. ORCID: 0000-0001-9239-3048

Wijnand IJsselsteijn is a Full Professor of cognition and affect in human-technology interaction at Eindhoven University of Technology (TU/e), scientific director of the Interdisciplinary Center for Humans and Technology at TU/e, scientific board member of the Eindhoven AI Systems Institute (EAISI), and part-time professor at the Jheronimus Academy of Data Science (JADS). He researches the impact of media technology on human psychology and the use of psychology to improve technology design. ORCID: 0000-0001-6856-9269

Bart A. Kamphorst is a Postdoctoral Researcher at Wageningen University & Research. He works on philosophical, ethical, and societal questions related to AI-driven behavior change technologies, particularly in the field of health. ORCID: 0000-0002-7209-2210

Llona Kavege is a Fulbright research fellow in the Netherlands based at Delft University of Technology and the University of Twente where she investigates the moral and social dimensions of partial-ectogestation. ORCID: 0009-0000-6074-3912

Michael Klenk is an Assistant Professor of ethics and philosophy of technology at Delft University of Technology. He works on the intersection of metaethics, epistemology, and moral psychology, and most recently on the topic of (online) manipulation. ORCID: 0000-0002-1483-0799

Dominic Lenzi is an Assistant Professor in environmental ethics at the University of Twente. His research focuses on ethics and political philosophy in the Anthropocene, including topics related to climate ethics, planetary boundaries and natural resource justice, and environmental values and valuation. ORCID: 0000-0003-4388-4427

Guido Löhr is an Assistant Professor of logic and AI at Vrije University Amsterdam. They work on various topics in philosophy of language, social ontology, and philosophy of technology with a focus on concepts. ORCID: 0000-0002-7028-3515

Björn Lundgren is a Postdoctoral Researcher at Utrecht University. He is working on methods of ethics of technology. ORCID: 0000-0001-5830-3432

Samuela Marchiori is a PhD candidate in conceptual engineering in the philosophy of technology at Delft University of Technology. She is developing methods to address and overcome the disruption of moral concepts in relation to socially disruptive technologies. ORCID: 0000-0002-6426-7690

Sven Nyholm is a Professor of the ethics of artificial intelligence at the Ludwig Maximilian University of Munich. His research explores how new developments in artificial intelligence and robotics are related to traditional topics within moral philosophy, such as moral responsibility, well-being and meaning in life, and our human self-understanding. ORCID: 0000-0002-3836-5932

Elisa Paiusco is a PhD candidate in philosophy at the University of Twente, where she investigates the social and ethical implications of carbon dioxide removal. Her work focuses on climate change and intergenerational justice. ORCID: 0009-0008-2369-294X

Giulia Perugia is an Assistant Professor at the Human-Technology Interaction Group of Eindhoven University of Technology. As a social scientist, her research lies at the intersection of social robotics, social psychology, and ethical and inclusive HRI. ORCID: 0000-0003-1248-0526

Ibo van de Poel is a Professor in ethics of technology at Delft University of Technology. His research focuses on values, technology and design and how values, and related concepts that address ethical issues in technology (can) change over time. ORCID: 0000-0002-9553-5651

Anna Puzio is a Postdoctoral Researcher of philosophy and ethics at the University of Twente where she works on the anthropology and ethics of technology, transhumanism, new materialism, robotics, reproductive technologies, diversity in AI, and environmental ethics. ORCID: 0000-0002-8339-6244

Patricia D. Reyes Benavides is a PhD candidate in philosophy of technology at the University of Twente. Her research delves into the technopolitics of the global climate movement, in particular the appropriation of internet platforms by climate activists. ORCID: 0009-0008-6867-864X

Julia Rijssenbeek is a PhD candidate in philosophy of technology at Wageningen University & Research. She investigates the philosophy and ethics of synthetic biology, focusing on the conceptual and normative shifts in thinking about biological matter and lifeforms that the field creates and their contribution to a bio-based future. ORCID: 0000-0001-7377-2667

Kevin Scharp is a Postdoctoral Researcher at the University of Twente. He has published widely on the topic of conceptual engineering. ORCID: 0000-0003-3900-4087

Behnam Taebi is Professor of energy and climate ethics at Delft University of Technology. Taebi is the co-editor-in-chief of *Science and Engineering Ethics*, and co-editor of *The Ethics of Nuclear Energy* (Cambridge University Press, 2015) and the author of *Ethics and Engineering. An Introduction* (Cambridge University Press, 2021). ORCID: 0000-0002-2244-2083

Elena Ziliotti is an Assistant Professor of ethics and political philosophy at Delft University of Technology. Her research focuses on Western democratic theory and comparative democratic theory, with a particular focus on contemporary Confucian political theory. ORCID: 0000-0002-8929-9728

Acknowledgements

This publication is part of the research program Ethics of Socially Disruptive Technologies (ESDiT), which is funded through the Gravitation program of the Dutch Ministry of Education, Culture, and Science and the Netherlands Organization for Scientific Research (NWO grant number 024.004.031).

Although this book has numerous fellows of the ESDiT consortium as authors, it also has been made possible by ESDiT fellows who did not participate as authors. In particular, we want to thank Ingrid Robeyns who contributed to the conception of this book and commented extensively on a near-final version, Peter-Paul Verbeek who contributed to the conception of this book, and Sabine Roeser and Joel Anderson who commented on earlier drafts.

We also thank Elisabeth Pitts of Open Book Publishers for proofreading and corrections, and Freek van der Weij for correcting references and text formatting.

The cartoons in this book have been drawn my Menah Wellen (www.menah.nl). Fig. 5.2 has been drawn by Ilse Oosterlaken.

Foreword

Technologies shape who we are, how we organize our societies, and how we relate to (other parts of) nature. Changes in technologies, and how they are implemented, can be profoundly unsettling. Social media is transforming conceptions of democratic politics; artificial intelligence challenges ideas about what is unique to humans; the possibility of creating artificial wombs may transform notions of motherhood and birth; and proposals for using climate engineering to address global warming may well reconfigure our responsibility to future generations and our relation to nature.

This book investigates how four technologies —social media, social robots, artificial wombs and climate engineering— can be socially and conceptually disruptive, and what new issues these raise, theoretically as well as practically. It discusses different modalities of conceptual disruption and possible responses, such as conceptual engineering (the deliberate revision of concepts for certain purposes). It argues that socially disruptive technologies raise new questions and may require new approaches and methods in philosophy.

This volume is the result of an intensely collaborative effort by members of the ESDiT (Ethics of Socially Disruptive Technologies) consortium, a large multi-year research program that is led by five universities in the Netherlands (University of Twente, Delft University of Technology, Eindhoven University of Technology, Utrecht University, and Wageningen University).

The ESDiT consortium aims to reassess, revise, and develop approaches in ethics and related philosophical subfields to deal with social and ethical challenges brought about by socially disruptive technologies (SDTs), such as artificial intelligence, robotics, synthetic biology, and climate technology. This book contributes to some of the key objectives of the ESDiT program as it proposes an understanding of conceptual disruption and discusses the disruptive effects of some key twenty-first century technologies. It also sets out that in order to adequately deal with socially disruptive technologies, there may be the requirement of developing new approaches for ethical assessment and guidance.

Although this book has many authors, the authors have worked from a focused set of shared themes and have employed agreed-upon definitions of key terms such as social and conceptual disruption. Chapters 2–5, which each discuss the disruptive potential of a specific technology (social media, social robots, artificial wombs, and climate engineering), have a consistent structure, and address the same questions: What are (potential) impacts and social disruptions brought about by this technology? How is this technology conceptually disruptive? What new questions and issues does this technology raise theoretically as well as practically?

We would like to thank all the members of the ESDiT consortium for making this book possible. This includes the authors of the various chapters, but also all the other fellows who have contributed to the research program as well as to the cooperative intellectual spirit in which a book like this became a real possibility. A special thanks goes to the lead authors who coordinated and edited the contributions to their respective chapters.

The Management Board of ESDiT
Current and former members:
Joel Anderson
Vincent Blok
Philip Brey
Julia Hermann
Sven Nyholm
Ingrid Robeyns
Sabine Roeser
Andreas Spahn
Ibo van de Poel
Peter-Paul Verbeek
Marcel Verweij
and Wijnand IJsselsteijn

1. Introduction

Lead author: *Ibo van de Poel*[1]
Contributing authors: *Jeroen Hopster, Guido Löhr,
Elena Ziliotti, Stefan Buijsman, Philip Brey*

Technologies have all kinds of impacts on the environment, on human behavior, on our society and on what we believe and value. But some technologies are not just impactful, they are also socially disruptive: they challenge existing institutions, social practices, beliefs and conceptual categories. Here we are particularly interested in technologies that disrupt existing concepts, for example because they lead to profound uncertainty about how to classify matters. Is a humanoid robot — which looks and even acts like a human — to be classified as a person or is it just an inert machine? Conceptual disruption occurs when the meaning of concepts is challenged, and such challenges may potentially lead to a revision of concepts. We illustrate how technologies can be conceptually disruptive through a range of examples, and we argue for an intercultural outlook in studying these socially disruptive technologies and conceptual disruption. Such an outlook is needed to avoid a Western bias in labeling technologies socially or conceptually disruptive, as this outlook takes inspiration from a broad range of philosophical traditions.

---

[1] All mentioned lead authors and contributors contributed in some way to this chapter and approved the final version. IvdP is the lead author of this chapter. He coordinated the contributions to this chapter and did the final editing. He also wrote the first version of Section 1.5. SB wrote a first version of Section 1.1. and contributed to and commented on several other sections. JH wrote a first version of Section 1.2 and further contributed mainly to Section 1.3. GL wrote a first version of Section 1.3. EZ wrote Section 1.4. PB contributed to some of the examples given in Section 1.3.

https://doi.org/10.11647/OBP.0366.01

Fig. 1.1 Conceptual disruption. Credit: Menah Wellen

1.1 Introduction

When the birth control pill was introduced in the 1960s, society changed (Diczfalusy, 2000; Van der Burg, 2003; Swierstra, 2013). Women could suddenly delay pregnancy or decide not to have children at all, whereas earlier methods such as Aristotle's cedar oil or ancient Egypt's crocodile dung never really offered women a choice. With the pill there was a choice, and sex became increasingly divorced from reproduction. As a result, family sizes changed. The introduction of the pill also had larger social ramifications, alongside other social factors. It became feasible to invest long periods of time in studying, without having to worry about children that needed to be cared for. The proportion of women studying subjects such as law and medicine rose dramatically briefly after the pill became available to unmarried women (Bernstein and Jones, 2019). Marriage practices changed as well now that prolonged dating was feasible. Everyone, including those not on the pill, married later. In short, a single invention changed not just our reproduction, but also wider aspects of society such as gender equality and sexuality. Technology has always had these profound implications for human beings and society and will continue to have them.

What's more, technologies don't just alter the way we behave. They can also change the way in which we think by challenging concepts and ways of dividing up the world that we had taken for granted. Consider an example that has been discussed in many recent works of ethics of technology: the notion of 'brain death', which emerged in response to the invention of the mechanical ventilator halfway the twentieth century (Baker, 2013; Nickel et al., 2022). As a result of this technology, situations could emerge where a person could retain a capacity to breathe and have a beating heart, yet lack any kind of responsiveness. These patients displayed features considered paradigmatic of being dead (a lack of behavioral capacities; a lack of brain activity), but also some features considered typical of being alive (a heartbeat) (Belkin, 2003). A medical committee discussed the implications of this new state and the medical norms that should be followed, including the ethics of organ transplantation (should this patient be treated as being dead or alive?). In the course of these discussions they considered various options about how these patients should be conceptualized, including redefining the concept of 'death', and assessed the ethical ramifications of various conceptual strategies. They ended up proposing the new notion of 'brain-death' — a new concept that emerged directly as a consequence of the new situation created by the mechanical ventilator.

Still other technologies challenge what is considered 'natural'. With the advent of geoengineering, also called climate engineering, the set of technologies that tries to solve some of the issues brought by climate change through deliberate intervention in the Earth's climate system, it is becoming less clear what 'nature' really is. If we can change the composition of the atmosphere and dim the light of the sun through technology, then where does the natural begin and the artificial end? Some have suggested that in the twentieth century we have been witnessing 'the end of nature' (McKibben, 1990). While such a claim may rest on a too simplistic notion of 'nature', and a too dualistic distinction between 'natural' and 'artificial', it nevertheless signals that something fundamentally is changing in the relation between humans and the living environment (Preston, 2012). When our actions change the environment so drastically, questions arise regarding whether we should allow the 'natural' course of things, where species go extinct and changing temperatures wreak havoc? Or should we adopt a notion of 'nature', in which we can control and steer it? Again, the advent of technology and the far-reaching implications of the new capabilities present some tough issues. Both in terms of how we ought to apply the technologies we have, and in terms of how we ought to think about entities such as nature, death, reproduction, and so on.

This new situation is the main concern of this book. How can we investigate and conceptualize the socially disruptive implications of new technologies? And how can we expand the ethical concepts, frameworks and theories that we use to assess these implications, and guide the development, implementation and use of these technologies?

We will discuss these issues in six chapters. This first, introductory chapter will introduce the notions of socially disruptive technologies and of conceptual disruption, and discuss them against the background of the philosophy and ethics of technology as they have developed so far. Chapters 2, 3, 4, and 5 will discuss four socially disruptive technologies, i.e., social media, social robots, climate engineering and new reproductive technologies, following a similar structure. Each of these chapters will start by analyzing the ways in which these technologies are socially disruptive: what are their implications for human beings, nature, and societies, and how can we investigate these impacts? We will then investigate the conceptual disruption that these technologies bring by focusing on the ways in which technologies challenge our understanding of humanity, nature, and society.

Furthermore, we will examine the disruption of ethical or normative concepts: which normative concepts are at stake, and to what extent do they need to be revised or expanded? Finally, these chapters will investigate the further implications of these social and conceptual disruptions. The final chapter of this book will draw some conclusions by explicitly addressing the theme of conceptual disruption and the need for conceptual engineering and conceptual change. What kinds of conceptual disruption can be envisaged? How can these disruptions be addressed? And what do they imply for ethical theory and for philosophy at large?

1.2 Impacts of technology and social disruption

We have discussed how a wide range of technologies can have a huge impact, both on how people behave and on how people think. Disciplines such as Ethics of Technology, Technology Assessment and Science and Technology Studies have long conceptualized this in terms of impacts. This might suggest that there is a one-directional and deterministic relation between the emergence of new technology and all kinds of social and environmental impacts. But, as empirical studies have shown, this relation is often more complex and haphazard (Bijker et al., 1987; Smith and Marx, 1994). For example, blockchain[2] is often portrayed as an energy-intensive but privacy preserving technology, but its actual impact depends on the purposes it is used for, and how it is exactly designed. It might be used for tax evasion (through electronic currencies like Bitcoin) but it can also help farmers in Africa with land registration (Mintah et al., 2020), and its energy use is highly dependent on how exactly it is designed (Sedlmeir et al., 2020). As this example illustrates, there are many choices that humans and societies make, or at least can make, on the path from the conception of new technological possibilities to actual impacts. In fact, one of the main tenets of current ethics of technology is that we should move ethical reflection upstream in this process, to the early phases of technological research and development, to avoid or mitigate moral problems upfront.

Despite the best efforts of ethicists and developers, we still feel an increasing impact of technology on our daily lives and societies. Sometimes for the better (as with the pill), and sometimes for the worse (as with social media), but often at a large scale that makes it worth calling these impacts social disruptions. What do we mean by 'social disruption'? The Cambridge dictionary defines the verb 'to disrupt' as '[t]o prevent something, especially a system, process, or event, from continuing as usual or as expected'. Similarly, the Merriam-Webster dictionary defines it as '[t]o break apart; to throw into disorder; to

---

2   Blockchain is a kind of digital database that allows storing data in blocks that are linked together in a chain. The individual blocks are cryptographically linked together after the newest block is verified and added to the chain. This makes it very difficult to tamper with the chain and makes any alterations to the chain permanent. It allows safely storing data with digital signatures but without central control.

interrupt the normal course or unity of; to cause upheaval in ... '.
Expanding on these definitions, social disruptions may be understood
as changes that prevent important aspects of human society (broadly
understood) from continuing without change, thereby generating
disorder or upheaval.[3] In the wake of a social disruption, business as
usual can no longer proceed: a rupture occurs that instigates substantial
social, institutional, existential, or ethical challenges.

Disruptions involve both a 'disruptor', i.e. whatever it is that instigates
the disruption, as well as an object of disruption. The disruptor may be a
single technology, but typically, it is better understood by considering the
wider context of sociotechnical systems, in which emerging technologies
play a distinctive role. Warfare and pandemics can be seen as disruptors to
human societies of the recent past, and emerging technologies have in turn
disrupted how we acted during war and pandemics. Think of the unmanned
drones used at the battlefront in Ukraine and the social media campaigns
instigated to win public sympathy or to discredit fake news during wartime.
Or consider the contact tracing apps and mass vaccination programs that
were instigated to curb the COVID-19 pandemic that disrupted human
societies globally. As these examples suggest, technologies often exert their
transformative potential as part of larger systems.

To be clear, we don't mean disruption here in the economic sense.
Scholars on disruptive innovation (especially Christensen, 2013) have
pushed the idea that new technologies can disrupt markets, creating
new kinds of products or services that make older companies obsolete.
That definitely has an impact, but the impacts we're critiquing are more
fundamental. Technologies can also affect strongly held values and beliefs,
core concepts, theories, norms, institutions and human capabilities. These
deep disruptions (Hopster, 2021) merit study at least as much as the
economic ones. Disruptions may occur in various domains, three of which
centrally figure in this book: the domains of the individual human, society,
and nature.

The domains of human, of society, and of nature are not neatly
delineated. Nonetheless, their distinction provides a useful starting point

---

3   In this book, we will also consider disruptions to nature and to non-human species
     as 'social disruptions' if they do not allow continuing as usual or cause disorder or
     upheaval. One may think of climate change or loss of biodiversity as an example of
     social disruption.

for thinking of the different levels and contexts in which technology may exert disruptive effects.

The human domain pertains to questions of human nature and human existence, as well as human capabilities, sensory experiences, and human self-understanding, all of which may be implicated by technology. Some scholars speculate that in the future, artificial womb technology may serve to decouple pregnancy from the (female) body (Enriquez, 2021). Obviously, such decoupling would also have major repercussions to human society.

The domain of society pertains to the quality of social life at a larger scale, including the cultural, institutional, and political practices that weave human social life together. An important concern at this level is that of differential disruption (Nickel et al., 2022): different groups may not be similarly affected by technological changes. For example, the use of artificial intelligence by commercial banks to make decisions about who receive a loan or mortgage may affect already underprivileged groups more than the average citizen because this technology may have a discriminatory bias (Garcia et al., 2023).

The domain of nature, in turn, extends to technological disruptions in the non-human realm, which affect other animals and the natural environment. Powerful new genetic technologies employing the CRISPR-cas9 gene-editing technique, as well as the perils of global warming and the resulting technologies that are contemplated and developed to stabilize the earth's climate, make disruptions in the natural domain a main topic of philosophical and ethical concern.

Deep disruptions challenge established natural boundaries, entrenched social categories, stable social and normative equilibria, as well as our conceptual schemes. They often engender deep uncertainty and ambiguity, as they make us lose our normative, theoretical, and conceptual bearings. Accordingly, deep disruptions call for reflection and reorientation. They require us not only to engage with new philosophical and ethical issues but also to rethink the very concepts and theories we use to think about these issues.

1.3 Conceptual disruption

This brings us to a core theme of this book: conceptual disruption. Concepts are the basic constituents of thought and theorizing. We use words and concepts to give expression to moral and social values, human capabilities, virtues and vices, as well as several other phenomena and features we deem morally relevant. At first sight, it seems that important concepts — agency, freedom, life, vulnerability, well-being, to name just a few (see Fig. 1.2 for a more extensive list) — are rather stable: philosophers may quibble about their precise meaning and application, but in outline their contents seem clear and fixed. But under closer scrutiny, this does not appear to be the case. Ethical concepts are frequently up for debate, and subject to uncertainty, as well as change. Some have even suggested that normative concepts are fundamentally contested (e.g., Gallie, 1955). We claim that technological development often plays a notable role in disrupting fundamental concepts — a role that has only recently been appreciated, but will be given pride of place in this book.

What is conceptual disruption? We take it to be a challenge to the meaning of a concept, which may prompt its future revision. Just as with other disruptions, it means that business as usual cannot continue. Our thinking has to change. Often this means that because of the disruption we are no longer certain how to apply a concept. We face classificatory uncertainty (Löhr, 2022), in the same the way doctors were not sure whether people with a heartbeat but without brain activity were still alive.

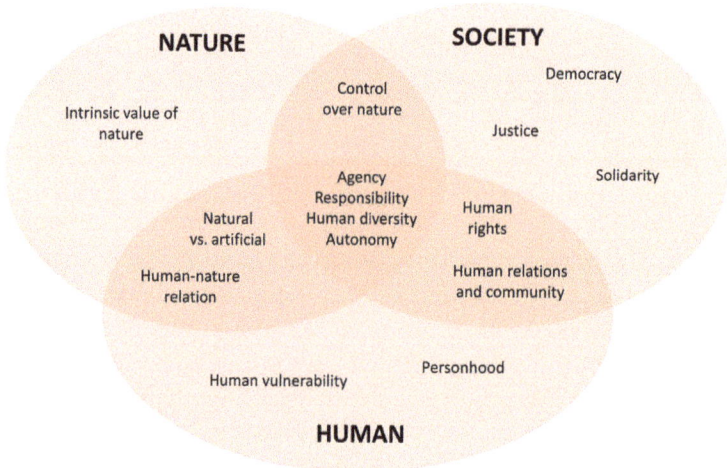

Fig. 1.2 Concepts in three domains that are studied in the ESDiT research program (Picture redrawn and adapted from original research proposal)

When technologies are conceptually disruptive, this may be an invitation to rethink the very concepts we use to comprehend and ethically judge these technologies. The conclusion of such reflection need not be a new concept or even a revision of existing concepts. It is equally possible that we have good reasons to retain an existing concept or to make it more precise.

Conceptual disruptions can come in different types (Hopster and Löhr, 2023). First, technological change may yield gaps in our conceptual repertoire. Such a *conceptual gap* occurs if a new technology yields artifacts, actions, relations, etc., on which we do not have an adequate conceptual grasp. In other words, existing concepts do not provide the needed descriptive or action-guiding tools; therefore, their revision or the introduction of new concepts is needed. Consider humanoid artificial agents like social robots and voice assistants that can evoke affective reactions (Nyholm, 2020; Lee et al., 2021; see also Chapter 3). People can feel upset when a robot is kicked or when a voice assistant is abused. Yet are such responses appropriate? They would be if the social robot and voice assistant were considered to be a 'person' or 'agent': after all, if a person is harmed, this calls for an empathetic response. Yet concepts like 'personhood' or 'agency' have traditionally been reserved for humans, and it is not yet established whether they can be extended to humanoid artificial agents, which may lack other relevant features of 'agency' and 'personhood', such as 'intentionality' or 'free will'.

One solution would be to extend attributions of 'personhood' and 'agency' to humanoid robots. But doing so also requires us to rethink what these concepts mean, and what their application conditions are, given the distinct characteristics of new digital technologies. Consider that at the same time, people have called for the responsible design of voice assistants: the fact that they often have female voices and continue to patiently respond and politely to harassment and insults could result in misogyny, and is therefore considered an undesirable design feature (Kudina, 2021; Nass and Brave, 2005; West et al., 2019). Thus humanoid robots simultaneously give rise to two rather different responses: an affective response, and an urge to design them as responsible and assertive agents. How should we deal with such entities, in descriptive and normative terms? Arguably, here we are confronted with a conceptual gap: we seem to lack a concept for entities that both evoke an affective response and that we should design in a responsible way.[4] For example, persons should be treated with empathy (and dignity), but it would seem improper to think of them as the object of responsible design.[5] Therefore, in order to account for the new roles of artificial agents, we need to recalibrate our concepts of 'personhood' and 'agency'.

Secondly, technological change may also give rise to *conceptual overlaps*. A conceptual overlap emerges when there is more than one concept that describes a new type of artifact, action or event. This might be unproblematic if two non-conflicting concepts apply, but in some cases conflicting concepts may seem to apply to one and the same artifact, action, or event. In turn, this may prompt us to decide as to which concept to apply. As an example, consider the traditional distinction between natural and artificial, and nature and artifact.[6] Particularly in Western conceptions of nature, there is a tendency to imagine part of the world untouched by human hands as natural, and picture human-made objects as artificial. Both concepts have various normative connotations. What is 'natural' is considered healthy, but also wild and dangerous, and what is 'artificial' might be less healthy, but is also safer and more regulated, and falls under the responsibility of human beings. However, very few things in the world are either fully natural or fully artificial, and those that are become more hybrid by the day. For example, few forests in the world are old growth forests; most are restored or newly planted forests that have been heavily influenced by human activity. Many animals and plants are the results of selective breeding. Recent

---

4   This assumes that both aforementioned responses are appropriate and normatively relevant. But one could also take a different stance and argue that our affective responses (and/or, perhaps, the appeal to responsible design) are misguided. In this case, one might instead want to speak of conceptual overlap. More generally, there seems room for different interpretations of examples in terms of conceptual gap, conceptual overlap and conceptual misalignment. For further discussion, see Chapter 6.

5   Technologies like CRISPR-cas9 might challenge the notion that humans cannot be designed. However, the genetic make-up of humans (that might perhaps be altered with such technologies) only partly determines their personality (nurture plays an important role as well). Moreover, it is questionable whether such design can be 'responsible' as genetic modification of humans is usually considered morally unacceptable.

6   Here we are mainly referencing Western folk conceptions of 'natural' and 'artificial'. There are, of course, much more nuanced and diverse conceptions to be found in the philosophical literature. Also note that some cultures do not have the natural-artificial distinction (IPBES, 2022). For further discussion, see Chapter 4.

developments in genetic engineering and synthetic biology make some organisms even more the subject of human design. Human-made artifacts tend to make use of organic materials and natural resources, with or without further processing. With the advent of geoengineering, even the climate may be partially brought under human control (see Chapter 4). Here, we seem to be confronted with a conceptual overlap because some entities — such as genetically modified tomatoes — are both 'natural' and 'artificial'. Perhaps the nature-artifact distinction is no longer useful, and the Western conception of the world might benefit from a new conceptual framework that does not fall into this simple dualism but instead is able to assess the world in a more nuanced way.

Thirdly, technological change that generates conceptual change may give rise to *conceptual misalignments*, i.e., situations where certain concepts are no longer aligned with our values and other concepts. Consider the concept of responsibility. Recent technologies, such as semi-autonomous weapons (drones) and self-driving cars, have raised questions about responsibility, and particularly the relation between control and responsibility. Traditionally, control is seen as a precondition for responsibility: without control, there is no responsibility (Sand, 2021). However, drones and self-driving cars are semi-autonomous and make their own 'decisions' independent from human operators; humans thus lack control and can seemingly not be held responsible. At the same time these systems lack reflective capacities and an awareness of their actions that we usually consider necessary to be responsible. Does this mean that we face a responsibility gap, where nobody is responsible for an action (Matthias, 2004)?

Consider military drones. The people ordering or overseeing a drone attack may lack control over it if the drone is programmed to autonomously decide what and when to attack. Suppose the drone mistakenly attacks a civil target, confusing it with a military target. Who is responsible for this mistake? Might we hold the commander responsible, or perhaps the designers of these systems? Maybe, but a broader issue seems at stake.

What we are witnessing here might well be a case of conceptual misalignment; the way we tend to think about responsibility (and control) in these cases might no longer align with certain values and moral convictions, such as the conviction that we should avoid responsibility gaps because their occurrence is undesirable. There are several ways we might resolve such misalignments. We may, for example, give up the moral conviction that responsibility gaps are always bad (Danaher, 2023). Another reply is the proposal for a new notion of control, so-called 'meaningful human control', that should ensure that autonomous systems remain under human control, so that humans remain responsible for them (Santoni de Sio and Van den Hoven, 2018). This latter might be seen as a form of concept revision (of 'control') in response to conceptual disruption (Veluwenkamp et al., 2022).

Or consider the concept of democracy. Democratic practices, such as elections, are increasingly influenced, if not undermined, by the use of social media technologies (see Chapter 2). But technologies like climate engineering may also raise questions about democracy. Such technologies may be extremely risky, not only for human beings but also for other living beings, and for entire ecosystems. How can we represent non-humans in democratic decision-making? Do they have moral rights, just like humans do? And how should we represent beings who are not alive yet, but who might experience the impact of climate engineering technology in the future? Upholding democratic decision-making might require us to expand our concept of the 'demos' that should be given power, and our notion of the democratic rights and duties that belong to the 'demos'. This might again be seen as a case of conceptual misalignment: it seems that the traditional notion of 'demos' may no longer align with the values we want to attain with 'democratic decision-making' and 'democratic representation'. Here, intercultural ethics might play a role in rethinking the concept of democratic representation. Ubuntu ethics, for instance, makes it possible to include ancestors and future generations in the moral community (Behrens, 2012; Pellegrini-Masini et al., 2020), while Maori ethics offers a basis to conceptualize the rights of ecosystems (Patterson, 1998; Watene, 2016).

As these examples demonstrate, technology has major potential to yield conceptual disruptions of various sorts. Technological change yields new entities, practices, and relations, which in turn call for the introduction of new concepts, or for rethinking and refining our current ones. Technological change may leave us with conceptual gaps, overlaps, and mismatches. In the face of these challenges, it is not enough to analyze the meaning of our concepts. Instead, we have to engage in normative and ethical reflection about the concepts we use to think about a rapidly changing world. These are the questions that conceptual disruption prompts and which we will address in the next chapters.

These conceptual changes resulting from technological change are often accompanied by shifts in values. The way we fundamentally think about the world is closely bound to what we find important in the world. So, when we change our concepts, this can have profound moral and social implications. Our value system is challenged, and this may result in profound changes in the way we evaluate the world and act on it (van de Poel and Kudina, 2022). For example, in the last century, we have witnessed the emergence of new moral concepts such as 'intergenerational justice' and 'planetary justice' (Hickey and Robeyns, 2020). Such concepts express new values and moral convictions, or at least values and moral convictions that have become much more prominent than in previous ages.

These new values and concepts, which express new responsibilities and obligations towards nature and future generations, may be seen as a response to the disruptive effect of certain technologies on the natural environment. However, while technology is a powerful instigator of conceptual disruption, it is not the only one. Concepts and conceptual schemes can also be challenged by other mechanisms. One such mechanism is intercultural dialogue. Conceptual disruption may occur through the interaction of communities that rely on somewhat different values, or on different ontologies. These prompt a rethinking of dominant concepts, and possibly a future revision of these very concepts. This is one of the reasons that underpins our emphasis, throughout this book, on the importance of intercultural philosophy in the ethics of socially disruptive technologies.

1.4 Intercultural outlook

What constitutes a social or conceptual disruption depends on the status quo, i.e., something is a disruption relative to a certain society, or certain practices, or a certain conceptual framework. However, too often, philosophers (of technology) have tacitly assumed their own society and their own conceptual framework as point of departure when talking about disruption. This issue has become more pressing than ever as more and more voices call for decolonizing and deparochializing the field of philosophy (Van Norden, 2017; Pérez-Muñoz 2021; Williams, 2020). We therefore have to ensure that when reshaping the way we think about the world in response to conceptual disruptions, we don't fall in the same trap of looking only at our own conceptual frameworks.

For decades, normative concepts and frameworks of thought derived from European historical experiences have dominated the international debate on philosophy and ethics of technology. This has led many students and scholars to assume that 'Western philosophy' is the definition of 'philosophy' and that Western normative paradigms apply universally to most human beings. However, for many, this modus operandi has become intolerable. Centering ethical and political discussions solely on issues affecting Western societies amplifies Eurocentrism. Furthermore, assuming that Western normative paradigms apply universally to the vast majority of human beings perpetrates coloniality — the epistemic repression intrinsic to colonial ideology (Wiredu, 1996; Mignolo, 2007; Quijano, 1992). The momentum of contemporary decolonising and deparochialising movements suggests that today's pressing question is not '*whether*' philosophical debates must be pluralized, but '*how*' to achieve this.

Although disruption is, in the following chapters, often discussed from a more Western perspective, we also pay attention to intercultural perspectives. An intercultural perspective helps prevent Eurocentric biases and fully understand technological disruptions' ethical implications. To the extent that the social consequences of the technologies discussed in this book affect the ways of life and social practices of inhabitants of both the Global North and South, an intercultural approach is key to assess this novel phenomenon appropriately.

There are two complementary strategies to pursue interculturality. One strategy uses experiences from a culture different from one's own to understand the magnitude of technology's social disruptions. This strategy contributes to decentering academic debates and helps uncover conceptual disruptions that would otherwise be harder or impossible to identify. For example, in Chapter 2, the analysis of social media in African societies is key to grasping the conceptual disruption that social media causes on the democratic idea of the public sphere. The dramatic situation of many African communities where public political debates unfold on foreign-owned digital infrastructure under very weak national institutional checks raises the question of whether the concept of public sphere is misaligned with the concept of demos. Viewed from this perspective, social media's disruption is broader than if it were viewed from a purely Western perspective.

The second strategy is to ask whether technology-driven social changes disrupt non-Western concepts and conceptual frameworks, in other ways than simply affecting Western philosophical discourse. This strategy contributes to the reorientation of the academic debates by increasing the relevance of non-Western philosophical concepts in contemporary philosophical theorizing and showing that Western conceptual frameworks are one among many possible alternatives. Thus, if the first strategy aims to change the terminology of the philosophical debate, the second strategy uses non-Western concepts to change the terms of the philosophical debate. For example, an Ubuntu perspective exposes new implications of social robots in Chapter 3. It reveals that if social robots crowd out human relations, this can impact our moral character and personhood, as these terms are understood within Ubuntu philosophy. In Ubuntu philosophy, interdependent relations are essential for personal cultivation. Thus, such a goal is harder to reach if robots crowd out human relations because humans cannot develop interdependent relationships with robots. Centering these terms as important, then, exposes the magnitude of this disruption.

Similarly, Buddhist traditions may help to overcome the inability of traditional Western ethical perspectives to articulate forcefully the full scope of some social disruptions, such as the character of our attention, which is transformed by new technologies (Bombaerts et al., 2023). In turn, this raises fundamental questions about how ethical practices of attention are related to self-control and willpower: the very idea of exercising control over one's thoughts is a fundamental moral issue within Buddhism, and this can inspire conceptual innovation in values such as responsibility and autonomy, as they relate to how we attend to others, ourselves, and the world.

By pursuing these two methodological strategies, we do not claim that this book presents an 'objective' understanding of technologies' conceptual disruption. Nor do we believe that the book is immune to

Eurocentrism. However, these two strategies can be a step forward in developing a more respectful and effective methodological basis for dealing with technology-driven conceptual disruption.

1.5 Expanding the research agenda of ethics of technology

The drive for more intercultural perspectives in the debate is part of a broader aim for the book, and the underlying research program ESDiT. We want to expand the research agenda of philosophy and ethics of technology. The point we want to drive home is that ethics of technology in the twenty-first century requires a conceptual turn by explicitly addressing social and conceptual disruption through technology, as well as attention to the question of when it is appropriate to revise concepts and how this should be done.

In philosophy, such questions about conceptual change have recently been addressed under the headings of 'conceptual engineering' and 'conceptual ethics'. We will discuss these approaches in more detail in Chapter 6. For now, the important point is that the advocated expansion of the research agenda of ethics of technology also implies closer collaboration between philosophy and ethics of technology and other subdisciplines of philosophy, like conceptual engineering, which explicitly thematizes how to adapt or ameliorate concepts. It also implies closer collaboration with philosophical disciplines that have traditionally developed and analyzed (core) concepts in the domains of nature, the human condition and society, such as philosophical anthropology, environmental ethics and political philosophy. In the past, these other subdisciplines of philosophy have often only paid scant attention to technology.

Ethics of technology has a long and fruitful tradition of collaborating with STEM disciplines, where STEM stands for science, technology, engineering and mathematics. Particularly since the 1980s, ethics of technology has developed from an emphasis on critique to an emphasis on more constructive, proactive and applied approaches. Oftentimes it is aimed not just at criticizing technology or putting a brake on technological developments, but rather at improving technological development by proactively addressing ethical issues and values in close collaboration with engineers, technology developers and policy makers.

Expanding the research agenda of ethics of technology also requires, we submit, new methods and approaches, for example for the ethical assessment of new technologies (Brey, 2012) or for addressing ethical issues and values through design (Friedman and Hendry, 2019; Van den Hoven et al., 2015). It may also have implications for other important themes in the ethics of technology such as the acceptability and management of technological risks (Roeser et al., 2012), moral responsibility (of engineers and others), social control and regulation of technology (Collingridge, 1980), the mediation of human perception and behavior through technology (Verbeek, 2005), and how to deal with (technological) uncertainty, to name just a few.

During the past few decades there has been increased attention on ethical issues brought about by specific technologies, which has led to the establishment of new fields of ethical inquiry. We now not only have computer ethics and bioethics, but also nanoethics, robot ethics, energy ethics, climate ethics, neuro-ethics, AI ethics, digital ethics, and so forth. While there is added value in specialized ethical inquiries into specific technologies, there is also a danger that larger themes go unnoticed and do not receive the theoretical treatment they deserve. This book therefore delves into the details of specific technologies in the following chapters, but does that in order to bring to the fore and to better understand a general phenomenon: the potential socially and conceptually disruptive character of new technological developments, and what new conceptual, theoretical and normative questions this raises.

Here we should not forget the dynamic interaction between technology, society and morality (Van de Poel, 2020). On the one hand, technologies reflect social choices and values, and therefore can be deliberately designed for certain positive moral values or to address ethical issues. On the other hand, technologies will not only raise new, sometimes unpredictable, ethical issues, but will also affect how people act and think, and what they consider desirable and undesirable. Mediation theory has argued that technology may change our perceptions and actions (Verbeek, 2005). For example, an echo of the fetus during pregnancy will affect people's perceptions of the unborn child, as well as their actions and choices. Others have pointed out that technology may induce technomoral change, i.e., a change in moral values, norms or routines that is triggered by technological advancements (Swierstra, 2013). This book takes the dynamic relation between technology, society and morality a step further by not just paying attention to the socially disruptive character of technology, but also by focusing on how technology may disrupt the very concepts by which we philosophically and ethically reflect on technology.

Further listening and watching

Readers who would like to learn more about the topics discussed in this chapter might be interested in listening to these episodes of the ESDiT podcast (https://anchor.fm/esdit) and other videos:

Jeroen Hopster on 'The nature of socially disruptive technologies': https://podcasters.spotify.com/pod/show/esdit/episodes/Jeroen-Hopster-on-The-Nature-of-Socially-Disruptive-Technologies-e19g3d8/a-a6pto8m

Olya Kudina on 'Voice assistants': https://youtu.be/ve6qJGt1_kk

References

Baker, Robert. 2013. *Before Bioethics: A History of American Medical Ethics from the Colonial Period to the Bioethics Revolution* (New York: Oxford University Press)

Behrens, Kevin Gary. 2012. 'Moral obligations towards future generations in African thought', *Journal of Global Ethics*, 8: 179–91, https://doi.org/10.1080/17449626.2012.705786

Belkin, Gary S. 2003. 'Brain death and the historical understanding of bioethics', *Journal of the History of Medicine and Allied Sciences*, 58: 325–61, https://doi.org/10.1093/jhmas/jrg003

Bernstein, Anna, and Kelly Jones. 2019. 'The economic effects of contraceptive access: A review of the evidence', *Institute for Women's Policy Research (IWPR) Report #B381*, https://iwpr.org/iwpr-issues/reproductive-health/the-economic-effects-of-contraceptive-access-a-review-of-the-evidence/

Bijker, Wiebe, Thomas P. Hughes, and Trevor Pinch (eds). 1987. *The Social Construction of Technological Systems: New Directions in the Sociology and History of Technology* (Cambridge: MIT Press)

Bombaerts, Gunter, Joel Anderson, Matthew Dennis, Alessio Gerola, Lily Frank, Tom Hannes, Jeroen Hopster, Lavinia Marin, and Andreas Spahn. 2023. 'Attention as practice', *Global Philosophy*, 33: 25, https://doi.org/10.1007/s10516-023-09680-4

Brey, Philip. 2012. 'Anticipatory ethics for emerging technologies', *Nanoethics*, 6: 1–13, https://doi.org/10.1007/s11569-012-0141-7

Christensen, Clayton M. 2013. *The Innovator's Dilemma: When New Technologies Cause Great Firms to Fail* (Boston: Harvard Business Review Press)

Collingridge, David. 1980. *The Social Control of Technology* (London: Frances Pinter)

Danaher, John, 2023. 'The case for outsourcing morality to AI', *Wired*, https://www.wired.com/story/philosophy-artificial-intelligence-responsibility-gap/

Diczfalusy, Egon. 2000. 'The contraceptive revolution', *Contraception*, 61: 3–7

Enriquez, Juan. 2021. *Right/Wrong: How Technology Transforms our Ethics* (Cambridge: MIT Press)

Friedman, Batya, and David Hendry. 2019. *Value Sensitive Design: Shaping Technology with Moral Imagination* (Cambridge: MIT Press)

Gallie, W. B. 1955. 'Essentially contested concepts', *Proceedings of the Aristotelian Society*, 56: 167–98

Garcia, Ana Cristina Bicharra, Marcio Gomes Pinto Garcia, and Roberto Rigobon. 2023. 'Algorithmic discrimination in the credit domain: what do we know about it?' *AI & Society*, https://doi.org/10.1007/s00146-023-01676-3

Hickey, Colin, and Ingrid Robeyns. 2020. 'Planetary justice: What can we learn from ethics and political philosophy?', *Earth System Governance*, 6: 100045, https://doi.org/10.1016/j.esg.2020.100045

Hopster, Jeroen. 2021. 'What are socially disruptive technologies?', *Technology in Society*, 67, https://doi.org/10.1016/j.techsoc.2021.101750

Hopster, Jeroen, and Guido Löhr. 2023. 'Conceptual engineering and philosophy of technology: Amelioration or adaptation?', Unpublished manuscript

IPBES. 2022. 'Summary for policymakers of the methodological assessment of the diverse values and valuation of nature of the Intergovernmental Science-Policy Platform on Biodiversity and Ecosystem Services (IPBES)', *IPBES Secretariat*, https://doi.org/10.5281/zenodo.6522392

Kudina, Olya. 2021. '"Alexa, who am I?": Voice assistants and hermeneutic lemniscate as the technologically mediated sense-making', *Human Studies*, https://doi.org/10.1007/s10746-021-09572-9

Lee, Minha, Peter Ruijten, Lily Frank, Yvonne de Kort, and Wijnand IJsselsteijn. 2021. 'People may punish, but not blame robots', in *Proceedings of the 2021 CHI Conference on Human Factors in Computing Systems*, Article 715. Yokohama, Japan: Association for Computing Machinery, https://doi. org/10.1145/3411764.3445284

Löhr, Guido. 2022. 'Linguistic interventions and the ethics of conceptual disruption', *Ethical Theory and Moral Practice*, 25: 835–49, https://doi. org/10.1007/s10677-022-10321-9

Matthias, Andreas. 2004. 'The responsibility gap: Ascribing responsibility for the actions of learning automata', *Ethics and Information Technology*, 6: 175–83, https://doi.org/10.1007/s10676-004-3422-1

McKibben, Bill. 1990. *The End of Nature* (Anchor Books: New York)

Mignolo, Walter. 2007. 'Delinking: The rhetoric of modernity, the logic of coloniality and the grammar of de-coloniality', *Cultural Studies*, 21(2–3): 449–514, https://doi.org/10.1080/09502380601162647

Mintah, Kwabena, Kingsley Tetteh Baako, Godwin Kavaarpuo, and Gideon Kwame Otchere. 2020. 'Skin lands in Ghana and application of blockchain technology for acquisition and title registration', *Journal of Property, Planning and Environmental Law*, 12: 147–69, https://doi.org/10.1108/ JPPEL-12-2019-0062

Nass, Clifford Ivar, and Scott Brave. 2005. *Wired for Speech: How Voice Activates and Advances the Human-Computer Relationship* (Cambridge: MIT Press)

Nickel, Philip, Olya Kudina, and Ibo van de Poel. 2022. 'Moral uncertainty in technomoral change: Bridging the explanatory gap', *Perspectives on Science*, 30: 260–83, https://doi.org/10.1162/posc_a_00414

Nyholm, Sven. 2020. *Humans and Robots: Ethics, Agency, and Anthropomorphism* (London: Rowman & Littlefield)

Patterson, John. 1998. 'Respecting nature: A Maori perspective', *Worldviews: Global Religions, Culture, and Ecology*, 2: 69–78

Pellegrini-Masini, Giuseppe, Fausto Corvino, and Lars Löfquist. 2020. 'Energy justice and intergenerational ethics: Theoretical perspectives and institutional designs', in *Energy Justice Across Borders*, ed. by Gunter Bombaerts, Kirsten Jenkins, Yekeen A. Sanusi, and Wang Guoyu (Cham: Springer International Publishing), 253–72

Pérez-Muñoz, Cristian. 2022. 'The strange silence of Latin American political theory', *Political Studies Review*, 20(4), 592–607, https://doi. org/10.1177/14789299211023342

Preston, Christopher. 2012. 'Beyond the end of nature: SRM and two tales of artificiality for the Anthropocene', *Ethics, Policy & Environment*, 15(2): 188–201, https://doi.org/10.1080/21550085.2012.685571

Quijano, Anibal. 1992. 'Colonialidad y modernidad-racionalidad', *Perú Indígena*, 13(29): 11–20

Roeser, Sabine, Rafaela Hillerbrand, Martin Peterson, and Per Sandin. 2012. *Handbook of Risk Theory: Epistemology, Decision Theory, Ethics, and Social Implications of Risk* (New York: Springer)

Sand, Martin. 2021. 'A defence of the control principle', *Philosophia*, 49: 765–75, https://doi.org/10.1007/s11406-020-00242-1

Santoni de Sio, Filippo, and Jeroen van den Hoven. 2018. 'Meaningful human control over autonomous systems: A philosophical account', *Frontiers in Robotics and AI*, 5: 15, https://doi.org/10.3389/frobt.2018.00015

Sedlmeir, Johannes, Hans Ulrich Buhl, Gilbert Fridgen, and Robert Keller. 2020. 'The energy consumption of blockchain technology: Beyond myth', *Business & Information Systems Engineering*, 62: 599–608, https://doi.org/10.1007/s12599-020-00656-x

Smith, Merritt Roe, and Leo Marx (eds). 1994. *Does Technology Drive History? The Dilemma of Technological Determinism* (Cambridge: MIT Press)

Swierstra, Tsjalling. 2013. 'Nanotechnology and technomoral change', *Etica & Politica / Ethics & Politics*, XV: 200–19

Van den Hoven, Jeroen, Pieter E. Vermaas, and Ibo Van de Poel (eds). 2015. *Handbook of Ethics and Values in Technological Design. Sources, Theory, Values and Application Domains* (Dordrecht: Springer), https://doi.org/10.1007/978-94-007-6970-0

Van de Poel, Ibo. 2020. 'Three philosophical perspectives on the relation between technology and society, and how they affect the current debate about artificial intelligence', *Human Affairs*, 30(4): 499–511, https://doi.org/10.1515/humaff-2020-0042

Van de Poel, Ibo, and Olya Kudina. 2022. 'Understanding technology-induced value change: A pragmatist proposal', *Philosophy & Technology*, 35: 40, https://doi.org/10.1007/s13347-022-00520-8

Van der Burg, Wibren. 2003. 'Dynamic ethics', *Journal of Value Inquiry*, 37: 13–34

Van Norden, Bryan. 2017. *Taking Back Philosophy: A Multicultural Manifesto* (New York: Columbia University Press), https://doi.org/10.7312/van-18436

Veluwenkamp, Herman, Marianna Capasso, Jonne Maas, and Lavinia Marin. 2022. 'Technology as driver for morally motivated conceptual engineering', *Philosophy & Technology*, 35: 71, https://doi.org/10.1007/s13347-022-00565-9

Verbeek, Peter-Paul. 2005. *What Things Do. Philosophical Reflections on Technology, Agency, and Design* (Penn State: Penn State University Press)

Watene, Krushil. 2016. 'Valuing nature: Māori philosophy and the capability approach', *Oxford Development Studies*, 44: 287–96, https://doi.org/10.1080/13600818.2015.1124077

West, Mark, Rebecca Kraut, and Han Ei Chew. 2019. 'I'd blush if I could: Closing gender divides in digital skills through education', *UNESCO*, https://en.unesco.org/Id-blush-if-I-could

Williams, Melissa. 2020. *Deparochializing Political Theory* (Cambridge: Cambridge University Press), https://doi.org/10.1017/9781108635042

Wiredu, Kwasi. 1996. *Cultural Universals and Particulars* (Indianapolis: Indiana University Press)

2. Social Media and Democracy

Lead author: *Elena Ziliotti*[1]
Contributing authors: *Patricia D. Reyes Benavides,*
Arthur Gwagwa, Matthew J. Dennis

Has social media disrupted the concept of democracy? This complex question has become more pressing than ever as social media have become a ubiquitous part of democratic societies worldwide. This chapter discusses social media's effects at three critical levels of democratic politics (personal relationships among democratic citizens, national politics, and international politics) and argues that social media pushes the conceptual limits of democracy. This new digital communication infrastructure challenges some of the fundamental elements of the concept of democracy. By giving citizens and non-citizens equal substantive access to online political debates that shape the political agenda, social media has drastically expanded and opened up the notion of demos and the public sphere (the communicative space where citizens come together to form and exchange opinions and define collective problems), and misaligned the conceptual relationship of the public sphere with the idea of demos. These conclusions have multiple implications. They indicate engineers' and designers' new political responsibility, novel normative

---

[1] All mentioned lead authors and contributors contributed in some way to this chapter and approved the final version. EZ is the lead author of this chapter. She coordinated the contributions to this chapter and did the final editing. She wrote the first version of Sections 2.3, 2.4 and parts of sections 2.2 and 2.1. PR wrote the first version of part of Section 2.2. and contributed to and commented on all the other sections. AG wrote the first version of part of Section 2.2. and contributed to, and commented on Sections 2.1 and 2.4. MD wrote the first version of Section 2.1 and contributed to the final editing of the chapter.

https://doi.org/10.11647/OBP.0366.02

challenges for research in political and moral philosophy, security and legal frameworks, and ultimately they shed light on best practices for politics in digital democratic societies.

Fig. 2.1 Voting machines. Credit: Menah Wellen

2.1 Introduction

Social media involves technologies associated with Web 2.0. Whereas Web 1.0 technologies divided *retrieving information* and *communication* into independent tasks, Web 2.0 technologies combine these processes. This gives rise to one of social media's quintessential features: hosting user-generated content which can be easily accessed and commented on by other users. Take Facebook's newsfeed, for example. This newsfeed combines the users' ability to comment on other users' posts, the algorithmic sorting of the content by recommender systems (i.e. microtargeting), and the ability of the post's author to comment on the reactions their post has generated.

These features of social media are now ubiquitous, but they are strikingly recent. *Six Degrees* is often credited as the first social media website. It was created a mere 30 years ago, in 1997. Despite this, social media now permeates many aspects of life such as work and career, dating, culture, spiritual wellness, friendship, and family relationships. Even governments often have social media pages, allowing users to get updates or to communicate with their members. Given the wide spread of social media, one might expect that social media has affected the democratic process and politics in general. For example, it is hard to imagine how a political election could occur today without significant use of social media technologies.

While social media has certainly added much value to today's political process, it also introduces new and unprecedented ethical challenges. It has the potential to improve both the quantity and quality of information that voters have at their disposal, allowing voters to share and communicate relevant information with other voters and facilitating political candidates' and other interest groups' communication with those they hope to persuade to vote for them. These opportunities for democratic engagement seemed to have multiplied when the first wave of widely used social media platforms by politicians grew exponentially in the early 2000s. Since that time, political parties who wish to represent traditionally disenfranchised voters could directly communicate with them. It was hoped that increasing interest in politics via social media would galvanize interest in the ballot box and other forms of civic activism. This can, for example, be seen in the run-up to the US presidential election in 2008 in which the Obama campaign made effective use of newly created social media accounts to mobilize many voters who previously had been politically disconnected (Smith, 2009).

Social media was not the only factor driving this. Obama's original political mandate and the progressive promise of electing the first Black president in US history played a vital role. Nevertheless, Obama's campaign made use of a growing interest in social media and targeting specific voters with relevant political content. However, the potential adverse effects of using social media in this way quickly became apparent. For progressives, the skillful deployment of these technologies by Obama's electoral team promptly turned into a cautionary tale.

Today's debates on social media and democracy spotlight the dual focus on the benefits and threats of technological developments. In particular, discussions often focus on the impact of algorithm decision-making systems in amplifying the scope of human action as well as their threats in conjunction with democracy, broadly understood in its deliberative form but also affecting individual and group rights such as privacy, expression, and association.

This chapter explores the relationship between social media and democracy from multiple perspectives. First, it dissects these interactive technologies' social disruptions in democratic societies (Section 2.2). We argue that social media's effects are visible at three critical levels of democratic politics: at the level of personal relationships among democratic citizens, at the level of national politics, and the level of international politics. These empirical reflections offer the background against which we explore social media's disruption of some of the fundamental elements of the concept of democracy (Section 2.3). We argue that as a new digital communication infrastructure, social media disrupts the idea of the public sphere, drastically exposing citizens' opinion formation to global political dynamics. Furthermore, quantitative and qualitative changes to the public sphere pose a conceptual challenge to our notion of demos, the very essence of democratic rule. Finally, we explore the implications of social media-driven disruption of democracy. This final section assesses the implications of social media-driven democracy's disruption for engineers' and designers' responsibility in society, for political and moral philosophy, for security and legal frameworks, and for political methodology (Section 2.4).

2.2 Impacts and social disruptions

What are social media's impacts and disruptive effects on democratic societies? As stated earlier, we identify this technology's impacts and social disruptions at three critical levels, starting with personal relationships among democratic citizens. In the past decade, researchers across disciplines have noted that social media has an unprecedented ability to radically change citizens' informational ecosystem. One important consequence is that social media transforms how users perceive political problems and formulate the political issues around them.[2] Such a process can have both harmful and beneficial effects on democracy. For instance, the platforms' algorithmic curation, which organizes the information in users' feeds, can distort users' understanding of the diversity of voices in a public debate, generating filter bubbles to increase users' engagement (Pariser, 2011). Then again, social media platforms afford the sharing of audio-visual content in real-time, which gives users richer insights into how others may be experiencing a common issue of concern.

Beyond how users may interpret political issues through social media platforms, these technologies disrupt the potential pathways for citizens' political engagement and action in democratic societies. The affordances of these technologies present citizens with new possibilities and limitations in their democratic practices. The possible ways for citizens to state their opinion, engage in public debates, campaign for a candidate or policy, bring awareness to an issue, or even mobilize fellow citizens have been disrupted by social media platforms. The shaping of these practices through technologies can be understood as a 'circumscribed creativity' (Zeng and Abidin, 2021) because it concerns how the features of various platforms define users' political practices in the digitalized public sphere. For instance, social media platforms' specific qualities shape how users can agree or disagree with a political stance. These features range from direct emoji reactions (e.g. the heart, sad, surprised, angry reactions on Facebook) to re-sharing, tagging, commenting, and the most recent remixing of original content (available on platforms like TikTok). Platforms may also limit content in terms of characters (when text-based) or time (when audio/visual-based). Therefore, they often push users to cram and communicate complex ideas in short bits. These examples of circumscribed creativity suggest that social media introduces distinct and qualitatively new ways for citizens' political interactions.

Although most literature on the role of social media platforms in democracy associates them with the power they wield in public life, just like in their nascent stage, they constitute places for users

---

2   This process has been coined *political hermeneutics* and it stems from an understanding of technologies as mediating their users' access to the world (Verbeek, 2020).

to connect, share entertainment, discuss popular culture, and stay in touch with each other's day-to-day lives. In private and public life alike, the platform algorithms shape how agents 'access information, communicate with and feel about one another, debate fundamental questions of the common good, and make collective decisions' (Simons and Gosh, 2020: 1). A nexus can therefore be observed between the roles of 'private' and 'public' in the life of a social media user. For instance, through nudges such as suggestions to like particular pages and befriend specific individuals, social media algorithms expand circles of human interaction and repertoire of choices, enabling freedom of expression, choice, and association, all fundamental to democratic decisions.

However, the same capabilities can also fragment users. The individual and group choices that occur in the context of the interplay between data and platform algorithms can give rise to new interactive social agents or algorithms. These, together with the technical rules that manage users' interaction with the other elements of the system, constitute sociotechnical systems (Van de Poel, 2020). However, the sociotechnical systems within social media platforms carry values, commercial motives, and political intentions. These do not just affect individual private decisions but can also influence society's ability to exercise collective decision-making.

This raises the question of social media's influence on democratic national politics, the second level of societal disruption we identify. What characterizes democratic government is citizens' more or less direct involvement in the decision-making process. However, for citizens to develop informed preferences that represent their actual needs and political views, they must have access to reliable and effective epistemic shortcuts and trustworthy information sources (Spiekermann and Goodin, 2018; Christiano, 2015). Because social media lowered the cost of information production and circulation, the number of sources on which citizens rely to form beliefs has significantly increased. As a consequence, the criteria through which traditional media established epistemic authority (e.g. editorial oversight, fact checking) have weakened (Farrell and Schwartzberg, 2021). For instance, the new communicative system allows virtually anyone on social media to be a publisher or a republisher (Farrell and Schwartzberg, 2021: 212).

This had both positive and negative consequences. On the one hand, it gave more voice to independent journalism and underrepresented and non-mainstream groups; on the other, it led to an increasingly polarized electorate (Sunstein, 2017). Debates about polarizing topics on social media tend to have low epistemic value, failing to achieve the 'wisdom of the crowd', (Sullivan et al., 2020) which has raised suggestions for new epistemic norms for sharing information online (Sullivan and Alfano, 2022). Algorithmic-based information selection can downgrade non-alarming material while directing users to more alarming information to maximize engagement (Farrell and Schwartzberg, 2021: 197). This polarizing effect is problematic for democratic national politics because, as we have learned, access to reliable and neutral information is critical for citizens to form beliefs and exercise their political rights in an informed way. Furthermore, polarization erodes the chances for constructive political debates. Changing the algorithm defining users' information visualization may limit social media's polarization effect. However, this is insufficient to address another troubling consequence of social media, which is that political leaders have acquired an unprecedented opportunity to directly reach out to voters bypassing traditional gatekeepers of democratic political communication, such as political parties (Makhortykh et al., 2021). Such consequence creates an unbalance of power by significantly increasing the political influence of political leaders while diminishing the relevance of political parties and other political agencies.

At this point, we identify the third level of social disruption in international politics: the transnational nature of social media platforms is challenging democratic states' ability to uphold digital borders alongside physical ones. The digital revolution, driven by the internet's diffusion and via social media platforms, has resulted in public discourses and criticisms becoming increasingly transnational with ramifications for various forms of democracy, whether deliberative or electoral.

With more than half of the world's population using global-reaching social media, communication across cultures has become more accessible and frequent (Boamah, 2018). This development has facilitated information dissemination, interpersonal communication, and the flow, sharing, infiltration, and transfer of various cultural elements worldwide

(Carey, 2008). Furthermore, this does not only apply to what individuals share themselves. The algorithms that empower social media create new forces that drive the flow of information in the public sphere (Simons and Ghosh, 2020). This leads the public sphere to become a cross-cultural discursive space, where strangers with little knowledge of each other's socio-cultural background rub shoulders.

Under such conditions, both dangers and advantages can be observed. On one hand, there is the potential for the intensification of conflict when different cultural backgrounds meet. Consider, for instance, the role that social media played in shaping the reaction to the terrorist attacks on the French magazine *Charlie Hebdo*. Sumiala, Tikka, and Valaskivi (2019) performed an analysis on the conversation unfolding on Twitter right after the incident became viral online. They found that the immediacy of reactions across the world (e.g. the global deliberation in 'real time') afforded by the platform incited users to make sense of the events through stereotypical narratives and mythologizations of cultural positions, arousing animosity between secular and Muslim groups.

On the other hand, the technological conditions that enable digital communication across cultures can also inspire necessary transcultural political action. Consider Iran's Green revolution, Hong Kong's Umbrella Movement (Liu, 2021), or Indigenous social movements such as the EZLN (Ejército Zapatista de Liberación Nacional), Idle No More, and the Rio Yaqui water rights movement (Duarte, 2017). These examples reveal the significance of digital tactics for local political organization, but they are also a testament to how social media has enabled cross-border solidarity. This is especially the case where such surges of political action touch upon issues and concerns widely shared across national boundaries, such as human rights violations, gender violence, wealth inequality, or climate change.

Notably, transnational mobilizations illustrate the disruption of older strategies for collective action. Transnational political mobilizations such as the Arab Spring, the Occupy movement and the more recent environmental networks such as Fridays for Future or Extinction Rebellion have brought to light the possibility of emerging collectives that did not need formal organization nor centralized resources to mobilize millions of citizens across nations and exert substantial political impact. Such phenomena have led some scholars to conclude that collective action was being substituted by *connective action*, a mode of mobilization characterized by digitally networked action in which social media enable individuals' personalized engagement and grant them freedom to interpret the collective's identity in accordance to each citizen's unique context (Bennett and Segerberg, 2013).

These considerations indicate that the transnational public sphere, now mostly centralized in private social media companies, has begun to play a significant role in shaping both local and global democratic politics. By facilitating an unprecedented global sharing of information and ideas, private social media companies own some of the most potent means by which active citizens in global civil society organize themselves today. Private social media platforms have become gatekeepers of expression that may excite contagious political emotions (Steinert and Dennis, 2022) and knowledge — or incite hatred, discrimination, violence, harassment, and abuse (Kaye, 2018). This raises significant worries because, for democratic institutions to endure, 'no entity, whether private corporations or social groups, could be permitted to acquire unfettered power to shape the public sphere or stifle the possibilities of collective action' (Simons and Ghosh, 2020: 2).

Helberger (2020) argues that instead of perceiving platforms as intermediaries and facilitators of the speech of others, they should be viewed as active political actors in their own right and wielders of considerable opinion power. Although Helberger and others make these claims in the domestic context, the impact and policy implications have been increasingly felt across national borders in the last decade, with the real danger of platforms becoming private sovereigns of the digital world to such a point of being accepted as political collaborators by governments (Cohen, 2019-a: 236; Cohen, 2019-b). Despite claiming a global status in their operation and normative influence, the platforms, primarily the US-based ones, resist falling under the governance of international human rights law. Jørgensen and Pedersen (2017: 95) maintained that in virtue of the importance of their services, corporations like Google have 'an extra obligation to respect human rights standards'. Although the activities of non-state actors are generally not governed by international law, except in limited instances, Article 19 of the International Covenant on Civil and Political Rights (ICCPR) applies in part to private actors such as businesses. For instance, according to the United Nations Guiding Principles on Business and Human Rights, private actors have the responsibility to respect international human rights. This includes avoiding causing harm as well as preventing and mitigating human rights impacts (UNHRC, 2011). The covenant rights apply whether there is an 'interference' with protected liberty or not. Specifically, under the gatekeeper theory, some intermediaries may have special responsibilities by virtue of their dominance, status, or influence on democratic discourse and democracy (Laidlaw, 2015).

2.3 Conceptual disruption

As illustrated in the previous section, social media has the potential to disrupt fundamental norms and practices both within democratic societies and between democratic societies and foreign actors (e.g. NGOs, foreign governments, multinationals, foreign private companies). However, social media's disruptive power is also conceptual; it can disrupt some of the core concepts through which philosophers and political scientists understand and assess democratic politics. As we saw in the introduction of this book, conceptual disruptions challenge the typically intuitive and unreflective applications of our concepts. This section evaluates how social media challenges critical conceptual elements of the idea of democracy.

Democracy is a complex and contested concept as philosophers have developed different conceptions of democracy (e.g. liberal democracy, representative democracy, deliberative democracy, participatory democracy, contestatory democracy). For the purpose of this chapter, it is important to consider two main kinds of conceptions of democracy: institutional and social. Institutionally, democracy refers to a set of institutions that aim to ensure the self-government of free and equal citizens. The institutional dimension of democracy is well represented by periodic general elections through which citizens can choose their political representatives. Socially, democracy stands for a way of life, a certain way through which members of the same society live together. This dimension of democracy is well-represented by a vibrant civil society. To make things more complicated, the ideal of democracy, no matter how contested this is, is also interconnected with various different concepts. This is already evident in the institutional conception of democracy, where the ideas of 'self-government', 'freedom', 'human rights', 'freedom of expression', and 'equality' are brought to the fore. Due to space limitations, this chapter focuses on two of the most fundamental conceptual elements of democracy: *democratic public sphere* and *demos*, and illustrates how social media destabilizes these two conceptual elements.

Among all conceptual elements characterizing the concept of democracy, the *public sphere* is the most critical concept that is challenged by social media. The idea of a public sphere is central to most conceptions of democracy; it represents the realm in which citizens develop their views on public matters and choose among options through communicative means of information transfers and exchange (Habermas, 1974). These public opinions, developed through deliberative public spaces, allow citizens to articulate collective problems and assess possible solutions. As a novel communicative infrastructure, social media gives the vast majority of democracy's citizens an unprecedented opportunity to participate in communicative political actions at almost negligible access cost and through a user-friendly structure. Of course, language barriers remain an important hindrance in some cases to a person's involvement in the politics of another country. However, as we have learned in the preceding section, adopting social media as a prominent avenue of communication among citizens has drastically extended democracies' public spheres beyond national borders.

This change represents a critical conceptual disruption of democracy. Although hardly any real social sphere has ever been free of international influences, the seemingly radical openness of the digital public sphere afforded by social media is genuinely unprecedented. Through these technologies, individuals outside of the geographies that usually delimit a democratic society have increasing opportunities to join the political discussions and conversations of citizens geographically located within the democratic community. This phenomenon has imposed a drastic expansion and openness of the public sphere, at the very least, quantitatively. Under these new circumstances, where national boundaries are blurred and geographical differences are irrelevant, where is the public sphere? Are there multiple public spheres, or is it more reasonable to talk about one unique global public sphere? In this regard, media scholar Ingrid Volkmer proposed to reconceptualize the fundamental aspect of the concept of public sphere to ensure that such concept is attuned and suitable for the political conditions brought by globalization (Volkmer, 2014).

Quantitative and qualitative changes to the public sphere also pose a conceptual challenge to another fundamental conceptual feature of democracy: *demos*. This Greek word initially referred to the political community or the citizens living within the democratic city-state who participate in the business of government. As democracy came to represent a political order of countries, the citizens' participation in government became more indirect, and the notion of demos came to refer to 'the people' or, more precisely, all the citizens of the democratic country.

The social disruptions laid out in the previous section challenge the conceptual limits of the concept of demos. We witness a conceptual misalignment between the concept of public sphere (international) and the concept of demos (national). The citizens of a given democracy are no longer the only agents who can significantly influence government business, considering the systematic openness of the digital infrastructure and the significant foreign political influences in the democratic political space and the increasing collaboration and solidarity among grassroots social movements across borders. These fundamental political changes raise the question of whether Abraham Lincoln's idea that a democracy is 'a government of the people, by the people and for the people' is achievable in the digital area. Can democracy be a government by the people, if citizens and non-citizens (e.g. single individuals but also private companies, NGOs, etc.) have equal access to the online political debates which shape a democratic society's political agenda? Of course, as we said before, this phenomenon is not unique to the digital age since hardly any real social sphere has ever been free of international influences. Democratic societies have always been decision-making systems open to foreign influences. But our point is not openness per se, but rather the unprecedented degree of this openness by virtue of social media and more generally the digital condition. This radical change is conceptually intriguing because it puts pressure like never before on the link between the concept of public sphere and the concept of demos.

The pressure on the conceptual limits of the concept of demos is critical for pragmatist and relational democratic theorists, who understand democracy primarily as a culture or way of life (Kolodny, 2014; Scheffer, 2014; Anderson, 1999; Anderson, 2009). For instance, according to John Dewey,

[A]merican democratic polity was developed out of genuine community life, that is, association in local and small centers where industry was mainly agricultural and where production was carried on mainly with hand tools. [...] The township or some not much larger area was the political unit, the town meeting the political medium, and roads, schools, the peace of the community, were the political objectives. The state was a sum of such units, and the national state a federation—unless perchance a confederation—of states. (Dewey, 1946: 111)

For Dewey, shared experiences developed in democratic community life are necessary for personal cultivation. But the globalization of valuable shared experiences through social media raises the question of whether democratic life as Dewey intended is still possible today.

This question is not only relevant for debates in Western political philosophy, but also for the prospect of non-Western democratic theories. For instance, within the field of Confucian political theory, several scholars, such as David Hall, Roger Ames, Tan Sor-hoon, and Sungmoon Kim, argue that while Western-liberal style democracy is incompatible with the Confucian tradition, Confucian intellectual traditions can support a conception of democracy as a way of life which is based on community-shared experiences (Hall and Ames, 1999; Tan, 2003; Kim, 2017; Kim 2018). These scholars have attempted to reconstruct a Confucian view of democracy precisely by emphasizing the striking normative similarities between Dewey's understanding of democracy and the Confucian belief that individual cultivation is primarily a community enterprise.

2.4 Looking forward

The disruptive effects of social media on democracy is pervasive and has four major repercussions: it has implications for engineers and designers' responsibility in society, for political and moral philosophy, for security and legal frameworks, and for political methodologies.

The expansion of the public sphere on digital platforms has made social-media engineers' and designers' choices politically laden. For example, consider the debates about whether fostering the original vision of a decentralized, open network or countering disinformation can be solved simply by implementing better algorithms or whether it requires governmental regulation. The pursuit of one of these choices could change how political debates are shaped and regulated. The same applies to decisions on other social media design features, such as the space limit of users' posts and users' ways of reacting to posts or storing content. As we have learned, these design choices have repercussions on how the citizens of a democratic society develop their political preferences. This is an important consideration, given that most of the debate on the philosophy of engineering has concentrated on the ethical responsibility of engineers, paying little attention to the political implications of engineering activities.

Some may argue that because engineers' and designers' choices are politically laden they must be controlled by democratic institutions representative of the citizens. On this point, Josh Simons and Dipayan Gosh maintain that since digital platforms provide the digital fora in which citizens learn and discuss politics, the discussion of Big Tech companies' key policy developments and implementations must involve citizens' juries (Simons and Ghosh, 2020: 14). While this participative proposal may be a partial solution, representative democracy allows for the presence of institutions that are insulated from direct electoral accountability if these agencies work towards democratic ends (e.g. the U. S. Supreme Court). From this perspective, it may be argued that the main reason for social media's negative influence on democratic politics may not be the lack of direct democratic accountability in Big Tech companies but rather the absence of effective regulation and uniform rules to define qualified information sources and epistemic authorities (Zuboff, 2019). Thus, one partial solution for democratic societies can be the development of public regulations for the privately-owned infrastructures of the digital public sphere while ensuring sufficient space for underrepresented voices. However, one challenge to this solution is that digital infrastructures cross national borders, connecting geographically distant users. Under these conditions, any democratic regulation risks being ineffective because it cannot regulate information production outside its national boundaries. Hence, an effective political response to the disruption of social media on national democratic politics can be only global.[3]

Besides implications for engineers' and designers' responsibility, social media's disruption of central conceptual elements of democracy (such as demos and self-government) has a significant impact on democratic theory. It indicates that scholars aiming at creating relevant normative models for contemporary democratic societies around the world must engage with the effects of technologies on contemporary democratic societies. Refusing to do so risks creating action guidance out of touch with how democratic politics works in reality. This conclusion is also relevant for political and legal philosophers whose research is not centered on democracy because social media's disruption extends to other fundamental political and legal concepts than democracy. Consider the division between 'private' and 'public' in the Western liberal tradition. On the one hand, there is the division between the universal public political realm, and on the other, there is the particular, private domain of needs and desires (Young, 2007: 108). However, the ability of social media to make public what traditionally were considered 'private' aspects of individuals challenges the liberal philosopher to rethink the dichotomy between the private and the public. Furthermore, social media platforms challenge political philosophers to rethink their distributive models of power and rights and examine the non-distributive issues of justice such as institutional decision making and culture, going beyond the distributive paradigm in favor of a broader, process-oriented understanding of society (Young, 2011: 33).

Social media-driven conceptual disruption is also relevant for moral philosophers. Social media challenges the practicability of some Western traditional conceptions of moral reasoning that seek to distinguish people's subjective lived experiences from the public, impersonal, and impartial ideals. By mediating ethical and political discourse among people from diverse backgrounds, social media challenges the basis of the Western traditional conceptions of moral reasoning where the rational agent arrives at a moral point of view by abstracting from the particularities of the circumstances in which moral reasoning occurs.

---

3   In response to this issue, David Kaye (2022) has argued that social media platforms should adopt global standards applicable across their platforms.

Furthermore, the discussion on social media's conceptual disruption indicates that social media disrupts fundamental political concepts and basic legal ideals. This has important implications for debates on security and legal frameworks. As we have seen, the transnational aspect of the new public sphere erodes the possibility of democratic self-government. From a legal perspective, this raises the question of whether social media has altered the fundamental concept of sovereignty. The transnational aspect of the public sphere hinders the ability of governments to provide security to their citizens from external influence. This does not have only negative implications; in some instances, the inability of governments to enforce their tight control has facilitated the protection of dissidents' human rights. For example, in January 2013, a form of 'WikiLeaks' under the handle Baba Jukwa was rapidly established as a major source of online political news in Zimbabwe. Operating under anonymity enabled by encryption, the handle published riveting reports about state corruption and was followed by over 100,000 people. Reportedly, the government undertook an intense campaign to find the poster's identity including approaching Facebook without success. According to Karekwaivanane, 'Baba Jukwa was able to convoke an "unruly public" that was situated in opposition to the state-controlled public sphere, and one that was transnational in its reach' (Karekwaivanane, 2019: 1).

Finally, the discussion on the social disruption of democratic politics by social media shows that social media has dramatically altered political methodologies. Not only has the digitalization of politics changed how many voters around the world form their political preferences, but it has also pressured other key political agents to adopt different strategies for political action. The use of social media by political leaders has pressured them into adopting different communicative strategies to reach out to voters and mobilize their supporters, critically affecting their agenda. Political activism too has gone through a significant transformation, as was described earlier through the new logic of connective action. The digitalization of politics has led political activists to adapt their demonstration and resistance tactics to maximize public outreach through the internet.

Further listening

Readers who would like to learn more about the topics discussed in this chapter might be interested in listening to this episodes of the ESDiT podcast (https://anchor.fm/esdit):

Elena Ziliotti on 'Confucianism and social media technologies': https://podcasters.spotify.com/pod/show/esdit/episodes/ Elena-Ziliotti-on-Confucianism-and-Social-Media-Technologies-e203lol

References

Anderson, Elizabeth. 1999. 'What is the point of equality?', *Ethics*, 103: 287–337, https://doi.org/10.1086/233897

——. 2009. 'Democracy: Instrumental vs. non-instrumental value', in *Contemporary Debates in Political Philosophy*, ed. by Thomas Christiano and John Christman (Chicester: Wiley-Blackwell), 213–27, ttps://doi. org/10.1002/9781444310399.ch12

Bennett, Lance W., and Segerberg, Alexandra. 2013. *The Logic of Connective Action: Digital Media and the Personalisation of Contentious Politics* (Cambridge: Cambridge University Press)

Boamah, Eric. 2018. 'Information culture of Ghanaian immigrants living in New Zealand', *Global Knowledge Memory and Communication*, 67(8/9): 585–606, https://doi.org/10.1108/GKMC-07-2018-0065

Carey, James W. 2008. *Communication as Culture* (New York: Routledge), https:// doi.org/10.4324/9780203928912

Christiano, Thomas. 2015. 'Voter ignorance is not necessarily a problem', *Critical Review*, 27(3–4): 253–69, https://doi.org/10.1080/08913811.2015.1111669

Cohen, Julie E. 2019-a. *Between Truth and Power: The Legal Constructions of Informational Capitalism* (New York: Oxford University Press)

——. 2019-b. 'Turning privacy inside out', *Theoretical Inquiries in Law*, 20(1): 1–31, https://doi.org/10.1515/til-2019-0002

Dewey, John. 1946. *The Public and Its Problems: An Essay in Political Inquiry* (Chicago: Gateway Books)

Duarte, Maria Elena. 2017. 'Connected activism: Indigenous uses of social media for shaping political change', *Australasian Journal of Information Systems*, 21, https://doi.org/10.3127/ajis.v21i0.1525

Farrell, Henry, and Melissa Schwartzberg. 2021. 'The democratic consequences of the New Public Sphere', in *Digital Technology and Democratic Theory*, ed. by Lucy

Bernholz, Helen Landemore, and Rob Reich (Chicago: Chicago University Press), 191–218, https://doi.org/10.7208/chicago/9780226748603.001.0001

Habermas, Jürgen, Sara Lennox, and Frank Lennox. 1974. 'The Public Sphere', *New German Critique*, 3: 49–55

Hall, David, and Roger Ames. 1999. *The Democracy of the Dead: Dewey, Confucius, and the Hope for Democracy in China* (Chicago: Open Court)

Helberger, Natali. 2020. 'The political power of platforms: How current attempts to regulate misinformation amplify opinion power', *Digital Journalism*, 8(6): 842–54, https://doi.org/10.1080/21670811.2020.1773888

Jørgensen, Rikke Frank, and Anja Møller Pedersen. 2017. 'Online service providers as human rights arbiters', in *The Responsibilities of Online Service Providers*, ed. by Mariarosaria Taddeo and Luciano Floridi (Oxford: Oxford University Press), 179–99, https://doi.org/10.1007/978-3-319-47852-4_10

Karekwaivanane, George Hamandishe. 2019. '"*Tapanduka Zvamuchese*": Facebook, "unruly publics", and Zimbabwean politics', *Journal of Eastern African Studies*, 13(1): 54–71, https://doi.org/10.1080/17531055.2018.1547257

Kaye, David. 2018. 'Report of the special rapporteur on the promotion and protection of the right to freedom of opinion and expression', *United Nations Digital Library*, https://digitallibrary.un.org/record/1631686

Kim, Sungmoon. 2017. 'Pragmatic Confucian democracy: Rethinking the value of democracy in East Asia', *Journal of Politics*, 79(1): 237–49, https://doi.org/10.1086/687762

——. 2018. *Democracy After Virtue: Toward Pragmatic Confucian Democracy* (Oxford: Oxford University Press)

Kolodny, Niko. 2014. 'Rule over none II: Social equality and the justification of democracy', *Philosophy and Public Affairs*, 42: 287–336, https://doi.org/10.1111/papa.12037

Laidlaw, Emily. 2015. *Regulating Speech in Cyberspace* (Cambridge: Cambridge University Press)

Liu, Jun. 2021. 'Technology for activism: Toward a relational framework', *Computer Supported Cooperative Work*, 30: 627–50, https://doi.org/10.1007/s10606-021-09400-9

Makhortykh, Mykola, Claes De Vreese, Natali Helberger, Jaron Harambam, and Dimitrios Bountouridis. 2021. 'We are what we click: Understanding time and content-based habits of online news readers', *New Media & Society*, 23: 2773–800, https://doi.org/10.1177/1461444820933221

Pariser, Eli. 2011. *The Filter Bubble: What the Internet is Hiding from You* (New York: Penguin Press)

Scheffler, Samuel. 2014. 'The practice of equality', in *Social Equality: On What It Means To Be Equal*, ed. by Carina Fourie, Fabian Schuppert, and Ivo Wallimann-Helmer (Oxford: Oxford University Press)

Simons, Josh, and Dipayan Ghosh. 2020. 'Utilities of democracy: Why and how the algorithmic infrastructure of Facebook and Google must be regulated', *Foreign Policy at Brookings and Harvard Kennedy School*, https://www.brookings.edu/research/utilities-for-democracy-why-and-how-the-algorithmic-infrastructure-of-facebook-and-google-must-be-regulated/

Smith, Aaron. 2009. 'The internet's role in campaign 2008', *Pew Research Center*, https://www.pewresearch.org/internet/2009/04/15/the-internets-role-in-campaign-2008/

Spiekermann, Kai, and Robert Goodin. 2018. *An Epistemic Theory of Democracy* (Oxford: Oxford University Press)

Steinert, Steffen, and Matthew James Dennis. 2022. 'Emotions and digital well being: On social media's emotional affordances', *Philosophy and Technology*, 35: 1–21, https://doi.org/10.1007/s13347-022-00530-6

Sullivan, Emily, and Mark Alfano. 2022. 'A normative framework for sharing information online', in *The Oxford Handbook of Digital Ethics*, ed. by Carissa Véliz (Oxford: Oxford University Press), https://doi.org/10.1093/oxfordhb/9780198857815.013.5

Sullivan, Emily, Max Sondag, Ignaz Rutter, Wouter Meulemans, Scott Cunningham, Bettina Speckmann, and Mark Alfano. 2020. 'Can real social epistemic networks deliver the wisdom of crowds?' in *Oxford Studies in Experimental Philosophy Volume 3*, ed. by Tania Lombrozo, Joshua Knobe, and Shaun Nichols (Oxford: Oxford University Press), 29–63, https://doi.org/10.1093/oso/9780198852407.003.0003

Sumiala, Johanna, Minttu Tikka, and Katja Valaskivi. 2019. 'Charlie Hebdo, 2015: "Liveness" and acceleration of conflict in a hybrid media event', *Media, War & Conflict*, 12(2): 202–18, https://doi.org/10.1177/1750635219846033

Sunstein, Cass. 2017. *#Republic: Divided Democracy in the Age of Social Media* (Princeton: Princeton University Press)

Tan, Sor-hoon. 2003. *Confucian Democracy: A Deweyan Reconstruction* (Albany, SUNY Press)

UNHRC resolution 17/4. 2011. *The UN Guiding Principles (UNGPs) on Business and Human Rights*, HR/PUB/11/04, https://www.undp.org/laopdr/publications/guiding-principles-business-and-human-rights

Van de Poel, Ibo. 2020. 'Embedding values in Artificial Intelligence (AI) systems', *Minds and Machines*, 30: 385–409, https://doi.org/10.1007/s11023-020-09537-4

Verbeek, Peter-Paul. 2020. 'Politicising postphenomenology', in *Reimagining Philosophy and Technology, Reinventing Ihde*, ed. by Glenn Miller and

Ashely Shew (Cham: Springer Nature Switzerland), 141–55, https://doi.org/10.1007/978-3-030-35967-6_9

Volkmer, Ingrid. 2014. *The Global Public Sphere: Public Communication in the Age of Reflective Interdependence* (Cambridge: Polity Press)

Young, Iris Marion. 2007. *Global Challenges: War, Self-Determination and Responsibility for Justice* (Cambridge: Polity Press)

——. 2011. *Justice and the Politics of Difference* (Princeton: Princeton University Press)

Zeng, Jing, and Crystal Abidin. 2021. '"#OkBoomer, time to meet the Zoomers": studying the memefication of intergenerational politics on TikTok', *Information, Communication & Society*, 24: 2459–81, https://doi.org/10.1080/1369118X.2021.1961007

Zuboff, Shoshana. 2019. *The Age of Surveillance Capitalism: The Fight for a Human Future at the New Frontier of Power* (New York: Public Affairs)

3. Social Robots and Society

Lead author: *Sven Nyholm*[1]
Contributing authors: *Cindy Friedman, Michael T. Dale, Anna Puzio, Dina Babushkina, Guido Löhr, Arthur Gwagwa, Bart A. Kamphorst, Giulia Perugia, Wijnand IJsselsteijn*

Advancements in artificial intelligence and (social) robotics raise pertinent questions as to how these technologies may help shape the society of the future. The main aim of the chapter is to consider the social and conceptual disruptions that might be associated with social robots, and humanoid social robots in particular. This chapter starts by comparing the concepts of robots and artificial intelligence and briefly explores the origins of these expressions. It then explains the definition of a social robot, as well as the definition of humanoid robots. A key notion in this context is the idea of anthropomorphism: the human tendency to attribute human qualities, not only to our fellow human beings, but also to parts of nature and to technologies. This tendency to anthropomorphize technologies by responding to and interacting with them as if they have human qualities is one of the reasons

---

1   SN is the lead author of this chapter. He coordinated the contributions to this chapter and, together with MD, he did the final editing of the chapter. SN wrote the first versions of Sections 3.1. and 3.3. and contributed material to all of the other sections. CF wrote the first version of Section 3.2. and also contributed material to Sections 3.3. and 3.4. MD wrote the first version of Section 3.4 and contributed to Sections 3.2 and 3.3. AP contributed material to all sections. GL contributed to Sections 3.1. and 3.3. DB contributed to Section 3.2. AG contributed to Section 3.4. BK commented on the whole chapter draft and suggested various edits to all sections. GP contributed to Sections 3.1 and 3.2. WI contributed to Section 3.3. All authors and contributors approved the final version.

     https://doi.org/10.11647/OBP.0366.03

why social robots (in particular social robots designed to look and behave like human beings) can be socially disruptive. As is explained in the chapter, while some ethics researchers believe that anthropomorphization is a mistake that can lead to various forms of deception, others — including both ethics researchers and social roboticists — believe it can be useful or fitting to treat robots in anthropomorphizing ways. The chapter explores that disagreement by, among other things, considering recent philosophical debates about whether social robots can be moral patients, that is, whether it can make sense to treat them with moral consideration. Where one stands on this issue will depend either on one's views about whether social robots can have, imitate, or represent morally relevant properties, or on how people relate to social robots in their interactions with them. Lastly, the chapter urges that the ethics of social robots should explore intercultural perspectives, and highlights some recent research on Ubuntu ethics and social robots.

Fig. 3.1 Social Robots. Credit: Menah Wellen

3.1 Introduction

While the expression 'artificial intelligence' comes from computer science, the word 'robot' comes from science fiction. The word was coined by a Czech playwright — Karel Čapek — in his 1920 play *R.U.R.*: *Rossum's Universal Robots*, which premiered in January of 1921, a little over 100 years before this book was written (Čapek, 1928; Nyholm, 2020). The robots in that play were similar to what many people still imagine when they hear the word 'robot' today: silvery/metallic artificial humans, or entities with a vaguely humanoid form, created to do work for us human beings. The robots in that play work in a factory. Towards the end of the play, the robots want their freedom and they want to know how to create their own robot children, so they do not have to depend on their human creators anymore. As it happens, the word 'robot' derives from the Czech language word 'robota', which roughly means 'forced labor'. The expression 'artificial intelligence', in contrast, was introduced in a 1955 research proposal for a summer workshop that took place at Dartmouth College in Hanover, NH, in 1956 — where the researchers proposed to create technologies that could 'simulate' all aspects of human learning and intelligence that could be precisely described (Gordon and Nyholm, 2021).

The development of robotics and artificial intelligence have both come a long way since 1920 and 1956 respectively, but not, perhaps, as far as many envisioned at several points in between then and now (Russell and Norvig, 2005; Dignum, 2019). These days, philosophers and others who write about or do research on robots typically do not mean artificial humans that work in factories when they use the word 'robot', though that is one of the ideas from science fiction that is still with us today (Gunkel, 2018). In fact, the tech entrepreneur Elon Musk presented a similar vision in August of 2021, when he presented his idea for the 'Tesla Bot' during a publicity event for Tesla. What he presented was the idea of a robot with a humanoid form that would work in Tesla factories, so that humans would not need to do that work anymore — a little bit like the robots in Čapek's play (Nyholm, 2023).

What do researchers who write and do research on robots now mean by the term 'robots'? And what are social robots? Many researchers are reluctant to give precise definitions of what one should understand by the word 'robot'. There are, they say, so many things that are called 'robots' that it is difficult to articulate what they all have in common; and if we follow some common definitions of what robots are, there are some things that qualify as robots, e.g., smartphones, that do not intuitively seem to be robots (Gunkel, 2018). Nevertheless, when researchers do offer definitions of what they mean by the word 'robot', they usually say something along the following lines: robots are embodied machines with sensors with which they receive information about their environment, and with actuators with which they can respond to their environment, in the service of certain specified tasks (Loh, 2019; Nyholm, 2020).

Researchers sometimes talk about the 'sense, plan, act' paradigm regarding how to understand what a robot is: it is a machine that can *sense* its environment, *plan* what it can do to achieve its task, and then *act* so as to achieve its task (Gunkel, 2018). A Roomba vacuum cleaning robot, for example, senses its environment as it moves around in a room; it detects obstacles (e.g., furniture in its way); and then it takes action so as to be able to continue vacuuming (e.g., moving around the furniture). A Roomba vacuum cleaning robot does not look like a paradigmatic robot out of science fiction. It looks more like a hockey puck or a beetle. But it is a robot by most common definitions of the term. In contrast, it is important to note here that the Roomba (by most accounts) is very limited with respect to its artificial intelligence. The two terms 'artificial intelligence' and 'robots' do not always pick out the same set of things.

A social robot is a robot that is designed to be able to interact with human beings in interpersonal ways (Breazeal, 2003; Darling, 2016). For example, a social robot might respond in a reactive/social way to touch, might have a chat function, or might in other ways respond to human interaction in the way a social being can be expected to. Such a robot does not have to look like a paradigmatic robot out of science fiction either (e.g., like the robots in the classic 1927 film *Metropolis*) but can take different forms. A well-known social robot is the robot seal Paro, which looks like a baby seal and responds to interaction with human beings in a way that appears interactive and soothing to some human beings. To give another example of a social robot from science fiction: R2-D2 from the movie *Star Wars* is a social robot.

Importantly, some social robots take on a humanlike form: a humanoid robot is a robot that is designed to look and behave like a human being

(Zhao, 2006; Friedman, 2022). The advantages and disadvantages of the humanoid form are discussed under the heading *anthropomorphism* (Friedman et al., 2022). Some humanoid robots reproduce the human body and behavior in subtle and stylized ways — as is the case for robots like NAO and Pepper. Other humanoid robots, instead, mimic the human body and behavior in extremely realistic ways — as is the case for robots like Geminoid HI-5 and Erica. These latter humanoid robots, which are conceived as robotic twins of existing (Geminoid HI-5) or imaginary persons (Erica), are called android and gynoid robots depending on whether they resemble a man or a woman. One well-known example of a gynoid robot is the robot Sophia from the company Hanson Robotics. Sophia is well-known, and controversial, for having generated various social responses in people, including being interviewed on popular TV shows (such as *The Tonight Show with Jimmy Fallon*), being invited to speak in front of the UN, and being named an honorary citizen of Saudi Arabia (Nyholm, 2020: 1–3).

Sophia and Hanson Robotics have been criticized by many technology experts and ethicists: the robot is deceptive, it has been argued, because it is presented as having a much more advanced form of artificial intelligence than it really has (Sharkey, 2018). Another controversial type of humanoid robot is the sex robot: robots created specifically for sexual purposes, but which are sometimes also presented as potential romantic companions for human beings, i.e., as not only being intended for purely sexual purposes (Richardson, 2015; Danaher and McArthur, 2017). The sex robots of today — usually a gynoid robot designed to closely resemble a human woman, though there are also prototypes that look like human men — are fairly rudimentary. But given how fast technological developments can be, it may be reasonably predicted that they and other forms of social robots might become extremely impressive and lifelike within the lifetimes of many of the people who are already alive today (Levy, 2008). We are not there yet, though (Nyholm, 2023).

Of related interest here are disembodied 'bots', such as Amazon Alexa, Siri, or Google assistant, or the chatbots that we interact with via chat windows in our browsers (any kind of customer service chatbots that filters customer complaints and decides whether to escalate an issue to a human). These bots are meant to interact with users through one-dimensional interactions (voice or text), and often maintain the artificiality of the interaction at the forefront. Even more impressive are the recently developed large language models using so-called transformer technology, like Google's LaMDA or OpenAI's ChatGPT, which specialize in what is presented as a form of 'conversation' with the user. Notably, LaMDA responds to inputs from users in an impressive enough way that one of Google's engineers, Blake Lemoine, famously went to the media to declare that he thought that LaMDA had become a 'sentient' 'person', who should be entitled to rights. To some commentators, the chat transcripts that Lemoine made public were not proof that LaMDA was conscious, but rather proof that these AI technologies will increasingly become able to deceive or at least confuse human users into thinking that they have more advanced properties than they already have (Bryson, 2022). In a sense, this can be seen as technologies that deskill humans with respect to the ability to tell the difference between fellow sentient beings and machines without a 'soul', another thing that Lemoine thought that LaMDA had.

One technology that has received less attention so far, but which is also of interest in this context, is the religious robot: social robots used in religious settings, which are particularly prevalent in non-monotheistic religions and the non-Western world. Religious robots attempt to mimic the spiritual and religious dimensions of being human. They can be used in a variety of ways and take on different functions. Religious robots could accompany religious rituals and ceremonies (e.g., the robot Pepper at funerals or Mindar reciting the Heart Sutra in a Japanese temple), bless (e.g. BlessU2), imitate religious conversations with patients in hospitals, recite Bible passages and religious narrations (e.g. SanTo), or engage in acts that are interpreted to bring luck, and offer protection. Thus, as social robots are increasingly developed, the question arises whether they will be presented as being atheistic, agnostic, or as belonging to a religion and having faith (Puzio, 2023).

Besides these more specific domains of application, social robots are increasingly used in education and healthcare — for instance, to help children learn higher-order thinking skills such as creativity (Elgarf et al., 2022) or to nudge people towards seemingly healthy behavioral outcomes (e.g., losing weight as in Kidd and Breazeal, 2008). As has been seen above, there is a wide range of social robots — either already in existence or in prototype form. In the future, it is to be expected that social robots will be used in an even wider range of domains of human life. At that point, many new ethical questions will arise about how we should interact with these robots. Yet already today, social robots — perhaps especially social robots with humanoid forms — raise ethical concerns and have the potential to be socially disruptive.

3.2 Impacts and social disruptions

Social robots are both impactful and socially disruptive. They force us to question the meanings of such concepts as sociality, care, relationships, relationality, and community, and more generally the issue of what constitutes social relationships (Zhao, 2006; Turkle, 2020). How is the relationship with a technology different from the relationship of humans to other humans or to animals? What makes relationships valuable, and do they necessarily rely on reciprocity? Below, different ways in which social robots might be socially disruptive or otherwise disruptive are described.

Social robotics researchers are often thinking about ways to improve social interactions between social robots and humans. Indeed, they study what makes humans enjoy interacting with social robots and accept them as social agents (Frennert and Östlund, 2014; Darling, 2016). To gain insights into what it means to engage in social behavior, researchers often turn to important components of human sociality. For example, mimicking other people's behavior is commonly understood to be an important part of human-human relationships, indicative of rapport building (Tickle-Degnen and Rosenthal, 1990). Due to this, some argue that social robots should also be capable of mimicry (Kahn et al., 2006).

Another key aspect to human sociality is reciprocity (Gouldner, 1960; Lorenz et al., 2016). Reciprocity is commonly understood as follows: '[W]e should try to repay, in kind, what another person provided us' (Cialdini, 2009). Or, put more simply: 'If you do something for me, I will do something for you' (Sandoval et al., 2016). Due to its importance in human relationships, robotics researchers have considered to what extent reciprocity should and can be implemented in social robots. Many claim that social robots should be capable of reciprocity (Kahn et al., 2006), pointing to empirical data that reveals that humans enjoy interacting with reciprocating computer programs (Fogg and Nass, 1997). However, others have pointed out that a seemingly reciprocal relationship between a human and a social robot is a deceptive relationship. Specifically, van Wynsberghe (2022) claims that a robot cannot engage in a truly reciprocal relationship. It is only using reciprocity to become more socially accepted by the human, and thus the relationship is founded on deception. Similarly, Robert Sparrow and Linda Sparrow (2006) argue that a relationship can only be meaningful when it occurs between social entities capable of reciprocal affect and concern.

Social robots are explicitly designed to draw upon people's fundamental social-relational capacities. Specifically, they are designed to draw upon the tendency that human beings have to *anthropomorphize*. The tendency to anthropomorphize is an evolutionary adaptation that people have to attribute human characteristics to that which is not human (Epley et al., 2007; Damiano and Damouchel, 2018). For example, humans tend to see faces in random patterns of objects or shapes (a phenomenon known as pareidolia) and tend to see social meanings in the movements of geometric figures (Heider and Simmel, 1944). When a child talks about her teddy bear being sad, the child is anthropomorphizing the teddy bear.

Anthropomorphization of social robots need not only come in the form of, or as a response to, physical appearance (cf., Sophia the robot or Ai-DA). Disembodied chatbots are examples of social robots or bots that we anthropomorphize, but not by designing them to appear human. Instead, we anthropomorphize them in the sense that we assume that they perform a very human action: they talk! In fact, most large language models of today, like Google's LaMDA or OpenAI's ChatGPT, simulate a conversation, but in fact only output a set of words that they compute as being the most likely to come next after a prompt, based on a huge amount of natural language data. This is clearly a very different kind of linguistic agent compared to a human conversational partner who has intentions, plans, and desires when she talks to you, and who can make commitments and take on obligations (Bender et al., 2021).

Traditionally, the tendency to anthropomorphize robots has been cast in a negative light (Bryson, 2010). It has been viewed as a 'bias, a category mistake, an obstacle to the advancement of knowledge, and as a psychological disposition typical of those who are immature and unenlightened' (Damiano and Damouchel, 2018: 468). However, social roboticists have seen the tendency to anthropomorphize as less of an obstacle, and more of a tool, which can be utilized to support and improve social exchanges between humans and robots (Gunkel, 2018). Research shows that people perceive computers and virtual characters as social actors (Nass and Moon, 2000). The embodiment and physical movement of robots further amplify this perception (Darling, 2016). As de Graaf (2016) explains, the physical presence of social robots and their capacity to speak and use humanlike gestures or facial expressions encourage people to interact with social robots as if they are human, and not simply a type of technology. Leveraging on this, roboticists have designed social robots to display emotions (e.g., facial expressions of happiness and anger), personality (e.g., introversion and extraversion), and even gender (Paetzel-Prüsmann et al., 2021; Perugia et al., 2022).

The magnitude of the potential effects social robotics may eventually have on social imagery, normativity, and human practices has led some researchers, such as Seibt (2016), to discuss the creation of social robots as a form of 'socio-cultural engineering'. For example, creating robots with apparent social skills, and thus making robots more like humans in their behavior, potentially comes hand-in-hand with the opposite tendency: encouraging humans to mimic robotic ways of doing things (Sætra 2022). Accordingly, the field of social robotics challenges socio-cultural sustainability, i.e. our ability to robustly maintain familiar cultural and social norms and practices (Gunkel 2023). The question arises of which of our human beliefs, norms, and practices that are rooted in tradition, culture, and social institutions are worth fighting for, even at the expense of technological innovation. According to Babushkina (2021a), social robotics in effect also brings us face-to-face with a problem of moral sustainability, i.e. 'the preservation of rationally justifiable moral values, norms, and practices' (Babushkina, 2021a: 305).

A reasonable goal in this context is to prevent a situation in which our moral practices change beyond what makes sense to us as human moral agents, rendering some of our interpersonal interactions absurd. Even though it might be difficult to grasp the elusive meaning of 'making sense', it is a fundamental need of a human being in her relationship to the world, be it co-existence with others, interaction with the environment, or experience of her own self. One of the main problems with social robots is that they get introduced as players into interpersonal relationships, i.e. the relationships that until now were only reserved for humans (e.g., companionship, friendship, parenthood, collegiality: Zhao, 2006). This means that social robots get plugged into various forms of intersubjectivity, apparently assuming the role of a partner in a relationship, but typically effectively failing to perform key functions that are morally required from the partner. What is significant from the moral-psychological point of view, for example, is that robots fail to meet expectations and answer reactive attitudes that we are justified to have towards partners in such relationships. This potentially leads to absurd experiences.

Following Wilks (2010), we can imagine a care robot presented as capable of ensuring the well-being of an elder, including giving her advice about weather-appropriate clothing. One day the companion gives the wrong information and the elder gets sick. You try to complain to the company, but it refers you to a small print where any blameworthiness is denied and users are advised to use the robot at their own risk. Such clashes between interpersonal expectations and robotic reality may create a dilemma: either to rethink moral responsibility so that it can accommodate artificial agents (e.g., Floridi and Sanders 2004; Sullins III 2006; Gogoshin 2021; Babushkina 2022) or limit the extent to which robots should be allowed to take on important roles associated with interpersonal relationships.[2]

Moreover, some have raised concerns that the implementation and use of social robots may negatively impact us should we allow them to crowd out human relationships. We are already seeing something similar occur in Japan, as some men there have shown less interest in starting relationships with human romantic partners, due to the possibility of instead having a 'virtual girlfriend' (Rani, 2013; cf. Nyholm, 2020: Chapter 5). Therefore, the possibility for this to occur with social robots as well is not all that far-fetched.

---

2   Another example of social robots challenging the fundamental attitudes underlying interpersonal relationships concerns respect. The stronger the need for seamless integration of robots into the interpersonal sphere, the stronger the demand will be for them to be respectful. However, trying to stretch the concept of respectfulness to artificial agents may lead to identification of respect with external behavioral expressions and atrophy of respect as an attitude based on inherent appreciation of human value (Babushkina, 2021b).

Scholars have approached this concern from various angles (Friedman, 2022). Some are worried that the relations we have with social robots may negatively impact our human well-being and quality of life. For example, in the context of care robots for the elderly, these social robots may negatively affect the well-being of the elderly, should they lead to a reduction of human contact, given the importance of human contact for stress reduction and the prevention of cognitive decline (Sparrow and Sparrow, 2006; Sharkey and Sharkey, 2012).

Moreover, Turkle (2011), in her discussion about the 'robotic moment', has voiced the concern that replacing human relations with robotic ones will lead to social isolation, given the illusory nature of human-robot relations. In the context of sex robots, for example, Nyholm and Frank (2019) argue that these robots may block off some people's relations with other people, and that this is something about which we should be concerned, given the premise that human-human relationships are more valuable than human-robot relationships. More generally, Danaher (2019) has argued that in forming relations with robots, people may be less likely to go out into the world and express their moral agency, which may lead to them being reduced to mere moral patients who passively receive the benefits that the technologies bestow.

Many researchers also worry that the relationships people form with social robots may negatively reinforce human stereotypes. In this context, Perugia and Lisy (2022) have noticed how the gender of a humanoid robot transforms the value of the interaction people have with it and might take on normative meanings for human society. For instance, using female robots in service and care-taking scenarios risks reinforcing normative assumptions about gender roles in society (Guidi et al., 2023). They invite roboticists to critically reflect on the ethical implications of gendering humanoid robots, especially considering the highly symbolic value of human-humanoid interactions for human-human relations.

3.3 Conceptual disruption

The way people respond to social robots places these robots in a confusing ontological space in society (Gunkel, 2023). Social robots are, essentially, a technological artifact, yet there is a tendency to perceive them as something more than this (Strasser, 2022). Specifically, social robots are blurring the line between being alive and being lifelike: we intuitively perceive them as being alive in some sense, although we are aware that they are not (Carpinella et al., 2017; Spatola and Chaminade, 2022).

Moreover, social robots challenge the boundaries between animate and inanimate, human, animal and machine, body and technology. They challenge the understanding of the human being anew. For example, in response to social robotics, we need to ask what emotions are, what constitutes action, what constitutes a relationship with the body. In the context of robotics more generally, questions also arise as to where the boundary between our human body and technology lies. Can technology be understood as part of the human body? Disability studies have shown that wheelchairs or prostheses are also sometimes perceived as part of one's own body. In a similar way, robots can potentially contribute to a broader, more inclusive understanding of the body (Thweatt, 2018; Graham, 1999; Puzio, 2022).

As we have seen in the introduction to this book, the uncertainty about which concepts we should use or apply when interacting with a new technological artifact is a form of conceptual disruption (see also Löhr, 2022). A conceptual disruption occurs if we either have no concepts to classify something or if two or more conflicting concepts seem to apply more or less equally well, such that we have to make a conceptual decision (is it dead or is it alive?). Such decisions are often difficult to make, but since we cannot leave objects uncategorized if we want to talk about them or act in relation with them, we often have no choice but to make a decision eventually.

Social robots can also have disruptive impacts on people's emotional lives. Some people have gone so far as to form deeply emotional social bonds with social robots, due to the perception that they are alive or in the possession of personalities. For example, in Japan, Sony's AIBO robots (which take the form of a dog) were honored with funeral ceremonies, when older models could no longer be updated. Although having 'doggish' behaviors, such as the ability to wag its tail, the AIBO robot also had human-like features, such as the ability to dance and, in later models, speak. Thus, many AIBO owners anthropomorphized these robots and subsequently formed deeply emotional bonds with them. As such, in 2014, when Sony announced that they would no longer support updates to older models, some AIBO owners perceived this message as a much more somber one: their pet robot dogs would die (Burch, 2018). In this same vein, the philosophers Munn and Weijers (2022) have recently suggested that when people get attached to technologies (such as the chatbot app Replika), this might create novel forms of ethical responsibilities for the tech companies behind these technologies, e.g., not deleting the apps, since this could be seen by some users as being a way of 'killing' their new friend (for further discussion, see Nyholm, 2023: Chapter 9).

The social response of perceiving these robots as being alive or as having a personality (and particularly humanlike) when they are not and do not, can be seen as ethically problematic or disruptive in the sense that human users are being deceived or even manipulated. Some argue that it is unethical to allow ourselves, or to cause others, to be deceived, if we assume that we have a duty to see the world as it is (Sparrow and Sparrow, 2006). In response to this, however, it has been pointed out that an animal using camouflage is a kind of deception, yet we do not find anything morally problematic about that (Sharkey and Sharkey, 2021). Moreover, sometimes deception has positive consequences, such as when baby dolls are introduced to people with dementia to help stimulate memories of a rewarding life role they once had (Mitchell and O'Donnell, 2013). Furthermore, the question arises as to when one should speak of deception as opposed to, say, make-believe. Children are raised with imaginary children's book characters, Disney film characters, and cuddly toys without this being considered deception or ethically reprehensible.

With these nuances in mind, Danaher (2020) argues that a form of deception wherein a robot deceives us into thinking it has a capacity it actually lacks is not necessarily ethically concerning. However, he does contend that deception in which a robot conceals the presence of a capacity which it does actually possess is seriously concerning. In the case of people with dementia — who are more likely to 'be unable to distinguish simulated or mediated reality from actual reality' — while there may be some positive consequences to using baby dolls to trigger certain memories, it does not take away from the fact that such dolls may be conduits of deception (Tummers-Heemels et al., 2021: 19). Thus, we should allow such instances of deception only 'sparingly, and with integrity and restraint' (Tummers-Heemels et al., 2021: 10).

Others, meanwhile, see robot deception as tolerable and even somewhat inevitable given the functions and purposes of the robots (Wagner and Arkin, 2011; Wagner, 2016). Indeed, just as humans sometimes use deception in their social interactions (such as when it is important to keep information private), it might be useful for a social robot to at least have the capacity to deceive. However until these questions are ultimately settled, it remains the case that conceptual disruption occurs. That is, these robots challenge our ordinary ontological distinctions between persons on the one hand, and things on the other. They seem to occupy some space in between these two extremes, at least with respect to how we intuitively respond to social robots (Strasser, 2022; Gunkel, 2023). Highlighting this form of ontological disruption lays a foundation for an understanding of why, and how, social robots are also potentially morally or, more broadly, conceptually disruptive.

Social robots not only encourage us to rethink our understanding of the human being; they are potentially also fundamentally changing anthropology. Anthropology as a field is increasingly turning away from essentialist conceptions of an imagined 'human nature' towards non-essentialist, dynamic, and fluid understandings of human identity. In particular, movements of thought such as New Materialism and Critical Posthumanism, which have been strongly influenced by the thinking of Donna Haraway among others, are striving to break down old anthropological concepts and dichotomies (of animate-inanimate, human-animal, human-machine, nature-culture/technology, woman-man). Haraway (1985) influentially discussed the ontological, epistemological, and political figure of the cyborg, which as a 'cybernetic organism' has a hybrid, fluid, and dynamic identity. The cyborg is neither unambiguously human, animal nor machine, thus refusing any categorization and classification and therefore maintaining subversive potential to resist any reontologization by humans.[3] Critical

---

3   The expression 'reontologization' here refers to the attempt to redefine what something is — i.e. to put it into a new or slightly different category in response to some new technological development or scientific discovery. Posthumanists tend to resist limiting definitions of what it is to be human, because they think that being human is open-ended, partly due to our 'cyborg'-like nature that is related to how we merge with the technologies we use.

Posthumanism and New Materialism thus reflect anew on notions of human, body, life, nature, etc. They draw attention to the fact that technologies such as social robots blur and question the above-mentioned boundaries and also seek to redraw these boundaries (Puzio, 2022).

The conceptual disruption of ontological concepts and categories caused by social robots also potentially creates a disruption of moral concepts and values, given the view that what an entity is, or is perceived as being, usually determines its moral status. Specifically, there may be a disruption in the context of our moral relations with social robots. Luciano Floridi (2013: 135–36) notes that 'moral situations involve at least two interacting components — the initiator of the action or the agent and the receiver of this action or the patient'. As Floridi sees things, robots can be moral agents but not moral patients. However, many authors who discuss the ethics of human-robot interaction disagree (for an overview, see Nyholm, 2021). They think that social robots can be both moral agents and moral patients. Moreover, the question arises as to what agency means and what it requires. For example, does agency presuppose consciousness? Some roboticists and philosophers — e.g. Asada (2019) and Metzinger (2013) — take seriously that it might be possible to create conscious robots. The well-known and influential philosopher of mind David Chalmers has even recently taken seriously the possibility that large language models might at some point become conscious.[4] However, this is controversial, and it also poses the difficulty that consciousness cannot easily be defined (Coeckelbergh, 2010a; Gunkel, 2018).

The different views about whether and why social robots can potentially be seen as moral patients can be divided into four broad classes, the first three of which relate the patiency of robots to their properties. These views can all be explained with reference to the following set of questions (Nyholm, 2023). The first question is: can social robots *have* morally relevant properties or abilities? Notably, most authors discussing this question are skeptical about the idea of current robots having morally relevant properties/abilities such as sentience or rationality/intelligence. However, some authors (e.g. Bryson, 2010;

---

4   In a presentation at New York University, Chalmers (2022) discusses the topic 'Are large language models sentient?'. Video available here: https://youtu.be/-BcuCmf00_Y

Metzinger, 2013; Schwitzgebel and Garza, 2015) think that it is possible to create social robots that could be conscious or have feelings and intelligence like human beings, and that such future robots should be treated with moral consideration.

Another question is whether robots can *imitate* or *simulate* morally relevant properties or abilities. This is perhaps more realistic. Danaher (2020), for example, focuses on this idea, and argues that if robots consistently behave like human beings with moral status behave, we should treat these robots with moral consideration, independently of whether we can establish whether anything is going on within their 'minds' (Coeckelbergh, 2010b). While Véliz (2021) argues that technologies can neither be moral agents nor moral patients because they are 'moral zombies' without consciousness or feelings, Danaher argues that what matters is instead whether they consistently behave as if they do. This is a kind of ethical Turing test, one could say.

Yet another question is whether social robots could *symbolize* or *represent* morally important properties or abilities. This expects even less of technology. Sparrow (2017; 2021) argues that robots and our interaction with robots represent various different morally important ideas, which means that how we treat, and interact with, robots is not morally neutral. In particular, Sparrow thinks that how we interact with robots — and how robots are made to appear to us — can represent various things that are highly problematic from an ethical point of view. Like Richardson (2015), Sparrow (2017) discusses sex robots as a key example of this, and they both think that human interaction with sex robots will almost inevitably represent morally problematic ideas — such as tropes associated with so-called rape culture. According to Sparrow (2021), while our interaction with robots could represent negative moral ideas, it is much harder — if not impossible — for human interaction with robots to represent or symbolize morally good ideas. Treating a robot 'well' cannot, Sparrow thinks, reflect well on a person, whereas treating a robot in a 'cruel' way (e.g. kicking a robot dog) can reflect poorly on us and our moral character.

A further type of view — which seeks to turn the idea of focusing on the properties or abilities of the robots on its head — says that the question we should be asking is not whether robots have, imitate, or symbolize morally relevant properties/abilities. We should instead be asking whether people *relate* to, or are disposed to relate to, (certain forms of) robots in ways that seem to treat the robots with moral consideration, and that welcome them into the moral community. Coeckelbergh (2010a) and Gunkel (2018) call this the 'relational' view of the moral status of robots. Chris Wareham (2021) defends a version of that view which appeals to the Ubuntu idea that 'we become persons through other persons'. According to Wareham, social robots can become persons through other persons, just like humans can: if the social robots are treated like persons and are welcomed into the moral community. Loh (2022) argues that a post-human perspective on human-technology relations favors this kind of relational view. According to Loh (2019), when somebody tends to treat a robot like a moral patient, a friend, or even a romantic partner, this is not a 'shortcoming' but a 'capability', which can be celebrated as part of human diversity.[5] Others, like Müller (2021), think that such views are deeply misguided. According to Müller, while we might wrong the owner of a social robot if we 'mistreat' their social robot (which the owner might presumably be attached to), we cannot wrong the social robot itself any more than we can wrong a pencil or a toaster — though here too we might wrong their owners if the owners are very attached to those.

Furthermore, the question arises whether this topic of moral agency, moral patiency, and the moral community is at all an appropriate and important question or whether discussion of this set of issues instead distracts people away from more urgent questions robot ethics should focus on instead (Birhane and Van Dijk, 2020). Gunkel (2023) points out that the debate shows that the right questions have to be asked, and that some authors might be asking the wrong questions or formulating their questions in misleading ways. Nevertheless, the very fact that such a varied debate about the moral patiency of social robots exists is indicative of the social and conceptual disruptiveness of the technology itself. Much as social robots create conceptual disruption with regard to our

---

5   Yet another way to approach moral patiency of social robots is through the concept of derivative vulnerabilities proposed by Babushkina and Votsis (2021). Their idea is that an artificial agent may be seen as acquiring a derivative right to persist depending on the degree of pairing with the user. This may happen when a computer device merges with the cognition of the user to such extent that they form a hybrid personhood, creating vulnerabilities, and mutual dependency of the user and the artificial agent.

uncertainty of how to ontologically classify them, so too the debate about the moral patiency of social robots shows that there is uncertainty about whether the concept of moral patiency is even applicable here (Löhr, 2022), especially since most technologies do not prompt such discussion. Moreover, we could also question whether (if we do indeed apply such a concept to social robots) the very meaning of what it is to be a moral patient may change, and whether it could alter the ways in which we apply the concept to ourselves. Could it even alter the way in which we perceive ourselves as moral patients in the world (Sætra, 2022)?

3.4 Looking ahead

In this final section, we briefly zoom out and look to the future. While a lot of interesting research has been carried out, there are still many opportunities when it comes to the future of social robots and their potential role(s) in society. Gaps need to be filled in, theories need to be further developed, and more diverse perspectives need to be taken into consideration. We are excited about the future, but we also urge caution, and in this last section we highlight some of the directions we see the field heading. We also make some brief recommendations about especially promising areas of new research.

Notably, in the future, it is to be expected that social robots will be used in an even wider range of domains of human life. This has implications not just for their technical design (i.e. their physical architecture and cognitive design) but also for the sociotechnical systems that underpin the various further potential contexts for social robots, as well as the ecosystems in which they will be deployed. On the technical side, there is likely to be increased convergence between social robotics and other developments in AI, such as generative AI, i.e. forms of AI that can generate new content out of the data they have been trained on, such as the large language model technologies discussed earlier.[6]

---

6   Regarding technical developments in robotics more generally, an interesting example here is how the COVID-19 pandemic generated interest in the potential of urban robotics and automation to manage and police physical distancing and quarantine in China (Chen et al., 2020). For discussion of development in drones, driverless vehicles, and service robots, see Macrorie et al. (2019) and While et al. (2020).

A key ethical question in relation to the potential introduction of social robots into more and more contexts is whether there are some contexts/domains where it is more problematic to make use of social robots than in others, and where it is better to avoid introducing social robots. In general, many new ethical questions will be raised about how we should interact with these robots in various settings, along with distributions of responsibilities as the robots become equipped with more advanced capacities and capabilities, and new hybrid intelligence systems are born, bringing further implications for sociotechnical systems design, across cultures (and generations).

Such developments have further implications. There is no guarantee that our traditional ethical norms related to human-human interaction will always carry over naturally to the ethics of human-robot interaction in all domains where social robots might come to be utilized (Nyholm, 2021). We may need to extend or update our current ethical frameworks in order to be able to tackle the new ethical issues that arise within new forms of human-robot interaction. Moreover, in addition to building on and extending traditional ethical frameworks from Western philosophy, we also see an increasing need for engaging with non-Western perspectives. Excitingly, some discussions are already taking such perspectives into account, such as those surrounding moral character.

In particular, there is a question about how the increasing prevalence of robots in human social relations could impact human moral character. For example, Friedman (2022) has contributed to this discussion by taking an ubuntu approach to the topic. Ubuntu places emphasis upon the importance of interdependent human relations, and, specifically on having other-regarding traits or characteristics within the context of these interdependent relationships (such as by exhibiting a concern for human equality, reciprocity, or solidarity). Such relations are important because they help us become 'fully human'. The notion of becoming 'fully human' is important because in Ubuntu philosophy we are not only biologically human, but must strive to become better, more moral versions of ourselves, in order to become fully human. Therefore, being fully human means being particularly moral in character. If robots crowd out human relations, this is morally concerning because we cannot plausibly experience an interdependent relationship with a robot, wherein other-regarding traits (such as human equality, reciprocity, or solidarity) are fully exhibited. Therefore, we cannot become 'fully human' i.e., better moral versions of ourselves, through relations with robots alone. Or so Friedman argues. This is concerning because should robot relations crowd out human relations, we would be interacting with human beings much less and, therefore, have less opportunity to develop our moral character in this way.

In addition to the Ubuntu approach, the dominant Western approach to robot ethics could also draw inspiration from Asian cultures, in particular, in South Korea, China, and Japan where many people place the perceptions of AI and robots at different points along the spectrum ranging from 'tool to partner' (Gal, 2020).

An interesting case, for example, is Japan, which has the highest percentage of industrial robots in the world (Kitano, 2015). The adoption of robots in Japan is partly based on Japanese Animism, 'Rinri' (in English, 'the Ethics'), in the context of Japanese modernization. Under this approach, the focus is on the harmonization of society, with each individual person forming a responsibility and accountability to that community. Within this culture, according to one interpretation, robots identify with their proprietor, and through such responsibility are just as accountable as their proprietor for the harmonization of Japanese society (Kitano, 2015). Conceptually, the Japanese approach could also be seen as a form of post-humanization — a distinct variant of posthumanism — which erases sharp human/non-human boundaries (Gladden, 2019: 8). In terms of social implications, under its Society 5.0 vision, Japan is promoting the integration of robots into society, and this is expected to contribute to society by presenting solutions to social problems, such as the labor shortages caused by the low birthrate and aging society, to enable every person to play a significant role by utilizing their own abilities (Japan Advisory Board on Artificial Intelligence and Human Society, 2017).

In general, how robots are received in society, whether they are accepted and how they are dealt with depends very much on cultural factors, which is why multicultural approaches to robots are important. Religions and other forms of worldviews also play an important role as cultural influences, as they shape value systems, understandings of nature and creation, as well as attitudes towards non-human entities, and thus also affect attitudes towards technology. There are major differences in the attitudes of religions towards technology, especially between the monotheistic religions and non-monotheistic religions which are historically more open towards a diverse range of attitudes towards objects and technologies (Puzio, 2023).

One area where we see room for further expansion is the discussion surrounding our obligations to robots. Notably, and partly due to their potential for significant social and conceptual disruption, Bryson (2010) warns against developing any kinds of robots that we would have obligations towards. Indeed, Bryson argued that we should only design robots that can be used as tools, to the benefit of humans. Following her lead, Nyholm (2020) contends that we should avoid creating humanoid robots in particular, other than if there is some very clear and morally significant benefit associated with certain forms of humanoid robots, such as in therapy. This will help us avoid running into moral dilemmas about how we should and should not relate to and treat robots.

How we think about our obligations to robots and what this means for the development of social robots will prove to have a significant impact on society at large. As such, we want to make sure that the benefits of developing social robots that we have obligations to outweigh the risks and costs. If we do not, we might end up putting ourselves into moral situations that we are not capable of dealing with, or develop technologies that we lose control over (for further discussion, see Nyholm, 2022).

With this in mind, we think that further research needs to be done in creating and developing a more moderate approach. That is to say, we do not think society should limit research on social robotics in the way Bryson (2010) seems to suggest, but we also want to make sure we tread carefully, with awareness of potential dangers and social disruptions. Thus, we call on researchers to come up with more suggestions on how to develop social robotics research in a responsible yet forward-looking way. For instance, there could be more of an emphasis on developing warning systems for social robots, which alert people to the particular capabilities of each robot (Frank and Nyholm, 2017). This would enable people to understand how best to approach and treat the robot, without needing to wrestle (quite as much) with moral and relational issues.

Beyond more design-oriented solutions, however, in order to appreciate the ethical disruption social robots set upon us and identify meaningful ways forward, we need to foster transdisciplinary research. Only by doing this can we encompass and fruitfully blend cross-disciplinary perspectives on social robots from diverse fields of knowledge, such as philosophy, anthropology, social science, psychology, design, computer science, and robotics, as well as the future individual users who will be the most affected by the introduction of social robots in society.

Further listening

Readers who would like to learn more about the topics discussed in this chapter might be interested in listening to these episodes of the ESDiT podcast (https://anchor.fm/esdit):

Cindy Friedman on 'Social robots': https://anchor.fm/esdit/episodes/Cindy-Friedman-on-Social-Robots-e19jnjc

Sven Nyholm on 'A new control problem? Humanoid robots, artificial intelligence, and the value of control': https://anchor.fm/esdit/episodes/Sven-Nyholm-on-A-new-control-problem--Humanoid-robots--artificial-intelligence--and-the-value-of-control-e1thcu1

Dina Babushkina on 'Disruption, technology, and the question of (artificial) identity': https://anchor.fm/esdit/episodes/Dina-Babushkina-on-Disruption--technology-and-the-question-of-artificial-identity-e1jstvm

References

Asada, Minoru. 2019. 'Artificial pain may induce empathy, morality, and ethics in the conscious mind of robots', *Philosophies*, 4(3): 38, https://doi.org/10.3390/philosophies4030038

Babushkina, Dina. 2021a. 'Robots to Blame?', in *Culturally Sustainable Social Robotics: Proceedings of Robophilosophy Conference 2020*, ed. by Marco Nørskov, Johanna Seibt, and Oliver Santiago Quick (Amsterdam: IOS Press), 305–15, https://doi.org/10.3233/FAIA200927

——. 2021b. 'What does it mean for a robot to be respectful?', *Techné*, 26(1): 1–30, https://doi.org/10.5840/techne2022523158

———. 2022. 'Are we justified to attribute a mistake in diagnosis to an AI diagnostic system?', *AI & Ethics*, 3, https://doi.org/10.1007/s43681-022-00189-x

Babushkina, Dina, and Athanasios Votsis. 2021. 'Disruption, technology and the question of (Artificial) Identity', *AI & Ethics*, 2: 611–22, https://doi.org/10.1007/s43681-021-00110-y

Behdadi, Dorna, and Christian Munthe. 2020. 'A normative approach to artificial moral agency', *Minds and Machines*, 30: 195–218, https://doi.org/10.1007/s11023-020-09525-8

Bender, Emily M., Timnit Gebru, Angelina McMillan-Major, and Shmargaret Shmitchell. 2021. 'On the dangers of stochastic parrots: Can language models be too big? 🦜', *FAccT '21: Proceedings of the 2021 ACM Conference on Fairness, Accountability, and Transparency*, 610–23, https://doi.org/10.1145/3442188.3445922

Birhane, Abeba, and Jelle van Dijk. 2020. 'Robot rights? Let's talk about human welfare instead', *Proceedings of the AAAI/ACM Conference on AI, Ethics, and Society*, 207–13, https://doi.org/10.1145/3375627.3375855

Breazeal, Cynthia. 2003. 'Toward sociable robots', *Robotics and autonomous systems*, 42(3–4): 167–75, https://doi.org/10.1016/S0921-8890(02)00373-1

Bryson, Joanna. 2010. 'Robots should be slaves', in *Close Engagements with Artificial Companions: Key Social, Psychological, Ethical and Design Issues*, ed. by Yorick Wilks (Amsterdam: John Benjamins Publishing Company), 63–74, https://doi.org/10.1075/nlp.8.11bry

———. 2022. 'One day, AI will seem as human as anyone. What then?', *Wired*, https://www.wired.com/story/lamda-sentience-psychology-ethics-policy/

Burch, James. 2018. 'Beloved robot dogs honored in funeral ceremony', *National Geographic*, https://www.nationalgeographic.com/travel/article/in-japan--a-buddhist-funeral-service-for-robot-dogs

Čapek, Karel. 1928. *R.U.R. (Rossum's Universal Robots): A Play in Three Acts and an Epilogue* (London: Humphrey Milford; Oxford University Press)

Chalmers, David. 2022. 'Are large language models sentient?', *NYU Mind, Ethics, and Policy Program*, https://youtu.be/-BcuCmf00_Y

Chen, Bei, Simon Marvin, and Aidan While. 2020. 'Containing COVID-19 in China: AI and the robotic restructuring of future cities', *Dialogues in Human Geography*, 10: 238–41, https://doi.org/10.1177/2043820620934267

Carpinella, Colleen, Alisa Wyman, Michael Perez, and Steven Stroessner. 2017. 'The Robotic Social Attributes Scale (RoSAS): Development and validation', *HRI '17: Proceedings of the 2017 ACM/IEEE International Conference on Human-Robot Interaction*, 254–62, https://doi.org/10.1145/2909824.3020208

Cialdini, Robert. 2009. *Influence: Science and Practice* (Boston: Pearson Education)

Coeckelbergh, Mark. 2010a. 'Robot rights? Towards a social-relational justification of moral justification', *Ethics and Information Technology*, 12: 209–21, https://doi.org/10.1007/s10676-010-9235-5

——. 2010b. 'Moral appearances: Emotions, robots, and human morality', *Ethics and Information Technology*, 12: 235–41, https://doi.org/10.1007/s10676-010-9221-y

Damiano, Luisa, and Paul Damouchel. 2018. 'Anthropomorphism in human-robot co-evolution', *Frontiers in Psychology*, 9: 468, https://doi.org/10.3389/fpsyg.2018.00468

Danaher, John. 2019. 'The rise of the robots and the crisis of moral patiency', *AI & Society*, 34: 129–36, https://doi.org/10.1007/s00146-017-0773-9

——. 2020. 'Robot betrayal: A guide to the ethics of robotic deception', *Ethics & Information Technology*, 22(2): 117–28, https://doi.org/10.1007/s10676-019-09520-3

Danaher, John, and Neil McArthur. 2017. *Robot Sex and Consent: Social and Ethical Implications* (Cambridge: MIT Press)

Darling, Kate. 2016. 'Extending legal protection to social robots: The effects of anthropomorphism, empathy, and violent behavior towards robotic objects', in *Robot Law*, ed. by Ryan Calo, A. Michael Froomkin, and Ian Kerr (Cheltenham: Edward Elgar Publishing), 213–31, https://doi.org/10.4337/9781783476732.00017

De Graaf, Maartje. 2016. 'An ethical evaluation of human-robot relationships', *International Journal of Social Robotics*, 8: 589–98, https://doi.org/10.1007/s12369-016-0368-5

Devlin, Kate. 2018. *Turned On: Science, Sex, and Robots* (London: Bloomsbury)

Dignum, Virginia. 2019. *Responsible Artificial Intelligence* (Berlin: Springer), https://doi.org/10.1007/978-3-030-30371-6

Elgarf, Maha, Natalia Calvo-Barajas, Patricia Alves-Oliveira, Giulia Perugia, Ginevra Castellano, Chirstopher Peters, and Ana Paiva. 2022. '"And then what happens?" Promoting children's verbal creativity using a robot', *2022 17th ACM/IEEE International Conference on Human-Robot Interaction (HRI)*, 71–79, https://doi.org/10.1109/HRI53351.2022.9889408

Epley, Nicholas, Adam Waytz, and John Cacioppo. 2007. 'On seeing human: A three-factor theory of anthropomorphism', *Psychological Review*, 114(4): 864–86, https://psycnet.apa.org/doi/10.1037/0033-295X.114.4.864

Floridi, Luciano, and Jeff Sanders. 2004. 'On the morality of artificial agents', *Minds and Machines*, 14(3): 349–79, https://doi.org/10.1023/B:MIND.0000035461.63578.9d

Floridi, Luciano. 2013. *The Ethics of Information* (Oxford: Oxford University Press)

Fogg, Brian, and Clifford Nass. 1997. 'How users reciprocate to computers: An experiment that demonstrates behavior change', *CHI '97 Extended Abstracts on Human Factors in Computing Systems*, 331–32, https://doi.org/10.1145/1120212.1120419

Frank, Lily, and Sven Nyholm. 2017. 'Robot sex and consent: Is consent to sex between a robot and a human conceivable, possible, and desirable?', *Artificial Intelligence and Law*, 25(3): 305–23, https://doi.org/10.1007/s10506-017-9212-y

Frennert, Susanne, and Britt Östlund. 2014. 'Review: Seven matters of concern of social robots and older people', *International Journal of Social Robotics*, 6(2): 299–310, https://doi.org/10.1007/s12369-013-0225-8

Friedman, Cindy. 2022. 'Ethical concerns with replacing human relations with humanoid robots: An Ubuntu perspective', *AI & Ethics*, 3 https://doi.org/10.1007/s43681-022-00186-0

Friedman, Cindy, Sven Nyholm, and Lily Frank. 2022. 'Emotional embodiment in humanoid sex and love robots', in *Social Robotics and the Good Life: The Normative Side of Forming Emotional Bonds with Robots*, ed. by Janina Loh amd Wulf Loh (Bielefeld: transcript), 233–56

Gal, Danit. 2020. 'Perspectives and approaches in AI ethics: East Asia', in *Oxford Handbook of Ethics of Artificial Intelligence*, ed. by Markus Dubber, Frank Pasquale, Sunit Das (Oxford: Oxford University Press) 607–24, https://doi.org/10.1093/oxfordhb/9780190067397.013.39

Gladden, Mathew. 2019. 'Who will be the members of society 5.0? Towards an anthropology of technologically posthumanized future societies', *Social Science*, 8(5): 148–86, https://doi.org/10.3390/socsci8050148

Gogoshin, Dane Leigh. 2021. 'Robot responsibility and moral community', *Frontiers in Robotics and AI*, 8(768092), https://doi.org/10.3389/frobt.2021.768092

Gordon, John-Stewart, and Sven Nyholm. 2021. 'The ethics of artificial intelligence', *Internet Encyclopedia of Philosophy*, https://iep.utm.edu/ethics-of-artificial-intelligence/

Gouldner, Alvin. 1960. 'The norm of reciprocity: A preliminary statement', *American Sociological Review*, 25(2): 161–78, https://doi.org/10.2307/2092623

Graham, Elaine. 1999. 'Words made flesh: Women, embodiment and practical theology', *Feminist Theology*, 7(21): 109–21, https://doi.org/10.1177/096673509900002108

Guidi, Stefano, Latisha Boor, Laura van der Bij, Robin Foppen, Okke Rikmenspoel, and Giulia Perugia. 2023. 'Ambivalent stereotypes towards gendered robots: The (im)mutability of bias towards female and neutral robots', *Social Robotics: 14th International Conference, ICSR 2022, Florence, Italy, December 13–16, 2022, Proceedings, Part II* (Cham: Springer), 615–26, https://doi.org/10.1007/978-3-031-24670-8_54

Gunkel, David. 2018. *Robot Rights* (Cambridge: MIT Press)

——. 2023. *Person, Robot, Thing* (Cambridge: MIT Press)

Haraway, Donna. 1985. 'A cyborg manifesto', *Socialist Review*, 80: 65–108.

Heider, Fritz, and Marianne Simmel. 1944. 'An experimental study of apparent behavior', *The American Journal of Psychology*, 57(2), 243–59, https://doi.org/10.2307/1416950

Japan Advisory Board on Artificial Intelligence and Human Society. 2017. *Report on Artificial Intelligence and Human Society*, http://ai-elsi.org/wp-content/uploads/2017/05/JSAI-Ethical-Guidelines-1.pdf

Kahn, Peter. Hiroshi Ishiguro, Batya Friedman, Takayuki Kanda, Nathan G. Freier, Rachel L. Severson, and Jessica Miller. 2006. 'What is a human? Toward psychological benchmarks in the field of human–robot interaction', *Interaction Studies*, 8(3): 364–71, https://doi.org/10.1075/is.8.3.04kah

Kidd, Cory, and Cynthia Breazeal. 2008. 'Robots at home: Understanding long-term human-robot interaction', *2008 IEEE/RSJ International Conference on Intelligent Robots and Systems*, 3230–35, https://doi.org/10.1109/IROS.2008.4651113

Kitano, Naho. 2015. 'Animism, Rinri, modernization; The base of Japanese Robotics', School of Social Sciences, Waseda University, http://documents.mx/documents/kitano-animism-rinri-modernization-the-base-of-japanese-robots.html

Levy, David. 2008. *Love and Sex with Robots: The Evolution of Human-Robot Relationships* (New York: Harper Perennial), https://doi.org/10.1109/MTS.2008.930875

Loh, Janina. 2019. *Roboterethik: Eine Einführung* (Stuttgart: Suhrkamp)

——. 2022. 'Posthumanism and ethics', in *Palgrave Handbook of Critical Posthumanism*, ed. by Stefan Herbrechter, Ivan Callus, Manuela Rossini, Marija Grech, Megen de Bruin-Molé, and Christopher John Müller (London: Palgrave Macmillan), https://doi.org/10.1007/978-3-030-42681-1_34-1

Löhr, Guido. 2022. 'Linguistic interventions and the ethics of conceptual disruption', *Ethical Theory and Moral Practice*, 25: 835–49, https://doi.org/10.1007/s10677-022-10321-9

Lorenz, Tamara, Astrid Weiss, and Sandra Hirche. 2016. 'Synchrony and reciprocity: Key mechanisms for social companion robots in therapy and care', *International Journal of Social Robotics*, 8(1): 125–43, https://doi.org/10.1007/s12369-015-0325-8

Macrorie, Rachel, Simon Marvin, and Aidan While. 2021. 'Robotics and automation in the city: A research agenda', *Urban Geography*, 42(2): 197–217, https://doi.org/10.1080/02723638.2019.1698868

Metzinger, Thomas. 2013. 'Two principles for robot ethics' in *Robotik und Gesetzgebung*, ed. by Eric Hilgendorf and Jan-Philipp Günther (Baden-Baden: Nomos), 263–302, https://doi.org/10.5771/9783845242200-263

Mitchell, Gary, and Hugh O'Donnell. 2013. 'The therapeutic use of doll therapy in dementia', *British Journal of Nursing*, 22(6), 329–34, https://doi.org/10.12968/bjon.2013.22.6.329

Müller, Vincent. 2021. 'Is it time for robot rights? Moral status in artificial entities', *Ethics and Information Technology*, 23(3): 579–87, https://doi.org/10.1007/s10676-021-09596-w

Munn, Nick, and Dan Weijers. 2022. 'Corporate responsibility for the termination of digital friends', *AI & Society*, https://doi.org/10.1007/s00146-021-01276-z

Nass, Clifford, and Youngme Moon. 2000. 'Machines and mindlessness: Social responses to computers', *Journal of Social Issues*, 56: 81–103, https://doi.org/10.1111/0022-4537.00153

Nyholm, Sven. 2020. *Humans and Robots: Ethics, Agency, and Anthropomorphism* (London: Rowman & Littlefield)

——. 2021. 'The ethics of human-robot interaction and traditional moral theories', in *The Oxford Handbook of Digital Ethics*, ed. by Carissa Véliz (Oxford: Oxford University Press), https://doi.org/10.1093/oxfordhb/9780198857815.013.3

——. 2022. 'A new control problem? Humanoid robots, artificial intelligence, and the value of control', *AI & Ethics*, https://doi.org/10.1007/s43681-022-00231-y

——. 2023. *This is Technology Ethics: An Introduction* (New York: Wiley-Blackwell)

Nyholm, Sven, and Lily Frank. 2019. 'It loves me, it loves me not: Is it morally problematic to design sex robots that appear to "love" their owners?', *Techné*, 23: 402–24, https://doi.org/10.5840/techne2019122110

Paetzel-Prüsmann, Maike, Giulia Perugia, and Ginevra Castellano. 2021. 'The influence of robot personality on the development of uncanny feelings', *Computers in Human Behavior*, 120, 106756, https://doi.org/10.1016/j.chb.2021.106756

Perugia, Giulia, Stefano Guidi, Margherita Bicchi, and Oronzo Parlangeli. 2022. 'The shape of our bias: Perceived age and gender in the humanoid robots of the ABOT database', *2022 17th ACM/IEEE International Conference on Human-Robot Interaction (HRI)*, 110–19, https://doi.org/10.1109/HRI53351.2022.9889366

Perugia, Giulia, and Dominika Lisy. 2022. 'Robot's gendering trouble: A scoping review of gendering humanoid robots and its effects on HRI', arXiv preprint arXiv:2207.01130, https://doi.org/10.48550/arXiv.2207.01130

Puzio, Anna. 2022. 'Über-Menschen', in *Philosophische Auseinandersetzung mit der Anthropologie des Transhumanismus* (Bielefeld: transcript Verlag), https://doi.org/10.14361/9783839463055

Puzio, Anna. 2023.: 'Robot theology: On theological engagement with robotics and religious robots', in *Alexa, Wie Hast Du's Mit der Religion? Theologische Zugänge zu Technik und Künstlicher Intelligenz*, ed. by Anna Puzio, Nicole Kunkel, and Hendrik Klinge (Darmstadt: wbg academic), 95–114.

Rani, Anita. 2013. 'The Japanese men who prefer virtual girlfriends to sex', *BBC News Magazine*, http://www.bbc.com/news/magazine-24614830

Richardson, Kathleen. 2015. 'The asymmetric "relationship": Parallels between prostitution and the development of sex robots', *SIGCAS Computers & Society*, 45(3): 290–93, https://doi.org/10.1145/2874239.2874281

Russell, Stuart, and Peter Norvig. 2005. *Artificial Intelligence: A Modern Approach* (Hoboken: Prentice Hall)

Sætra, Henrik. 2022. 'Robotomorphy: Becoming our creations', *AI & Ethics*, 2(1): 5–13, https://doi.org/10.1007/s43681-021-00092-x

Sandoval, Eduardo Benítez, Jürgen Brandstetter, Mohammad Obaid, and Christoph Bartneck. 2016. 'Reciprocity in human-robot interaction: A quantitative approach through the prisoner's dilemma and the ultimatum game', *International Journal of Social Robotics*, 8(2): 303–17, https://doi.org/10.1007/s12369-015-0323-x

Seibt, Johanna. 2016. 'Integrative social robotics—a new method paradigm to solve the description problem and the regulation problem?', in *What Social Robots Can and Should Do. Proceedings of Robophilosophy 2016*, ed. by Johanna Seibt, Marco Nørskov, and Søren Schack Andersen (Amsterdam: IOS Press), 104–15, https://doi.org/10.3233/978-1-61499-708-5-104

Schwitzgebel, Eric, and Mara Garza. 2015. 'A defense of the rights of artificial intelligences', *Midwest Studies in Philosophy*, 39(1): 98–119, https://doi.org/10.1111/misp.12032

Sharkey, Noel. 2018. 'Mama Mia, it's Sophia: A show robot or dangerous platform to mislead?', *Forbes*, https://www.forbes.com/sites/noelsharkey/2018/11/17/mama-mia-its-sophia-a-show-robot-or-dangerous-platform-to-mislead/

Sharkey, Amanda, and Noel Sharkey. 2012. 'Granny and the robots: Ethical issues in robot care for the elderly', *Ethics and Information Technology*, 14: 27–40, https://doi.org/10.1007/s10676-010-9234-6

Sharkey, Amanda, and Noel Sharkey. 2021. 'We need to talk about deception in social robotics!', *Ethics and Information Technology*, 23: 309–16, https://doi.org/10.1007/s10676-010-9234-6

Sparrow, Robert, and Linda Sparrow. 2006. 'In the hands of machines? The future of aged care', *Minds and Machines*, 16: 141–61, https://doi.org/10.1007/s11023-006-9030-6

Sparrow, Robert. 2017. 'Robots, rape, and representation', *International Journal of Social Robotics*, 9(4): 465–77, https://doi.org/10.1007/s12369-017-0413-z

——. 2021. 'Virtue and vice in our relationships with robots: Is there an asymmetry and how might it be explained?', *International Journal of Social Robotics*, 13(1): 23–29, https://doi.org/10.1007/s12369-020-00631-2

Spatola, Nicolas, and Thierry Chaminade. 2022. 'Cognitive load increases anthropomorphism of humanoid robots. The automatic path of anthropomorphism', *International Journal of Human-Computer Studies*, 167: 102884, https://doi.org/10.1016/j.ijhcs.2022.102884

Strasser, Anna. 2022. 'Distributed responsibility in human-machine interactions', *AI & Ethics*, 2: 523–32, https://doi.org/10.1007/s43681-021-00109-5

Sullins III, John. P. 2006. 'When is a robot a moral agent?', *The International Review of Information Ethics* 6: 23–30, https://doi.org/10.29173/irie136

Thweatt, Jennifer. 2018. 'Cyborg-Christus: Transhumanismus und die Heiligkeit des Körpers', in *Designobjekt Mensch. Die Agenda des Transhumanismus auf dem Prüfstand*, ed. by Benedikt Göcke and Frank Meier-Hamidi (Freiburg: Herder), 363–76

Tickle-Degnen, Linda, and Robert Rosenthal. 1990. 'The nature of rapport and its nonverbal correlates', *Psychological Inquiry*, 1(4): 285–93, https://doi.org/10.1207/s15327965pli0104_1

Tummers-Heemels, Ans, Rens Brankaert, and Wijnand Ijsselsteijn. 2021. 'Between benevolent lies and harmful deception: Reflecting on ethical challenges in dementia care technology', *Annual Review of CyberTherapy and Telemedicine*, 19: 15–20.

Turkle, Sherry. 2011. *Alone Together: Why We Expect More from Technology and Less from Each Other* (New York: Basic Books)

——. 2020. 'A nascent robotics culture: New complicities for companionship', in *Machine Ethics and Robot Ethics*, ed. by Wendell Wallach and Peter Asaro (London: Routledge, 107–16), https://doi.org/10.4324/9781003074991

Véliz, Carissa. 2021. 'Moral zombies: Why algorithms are not moral agents', *AI & Society*, 36: 487–97, https://doi.org/10.1007/s00146-021-01189-x

Van Wynsberghe, Aimee. 2022. 'Social robots and the risks to reciprocity', *AI & Society*, 37: 479–85, https://doi.org/10.1007/s00146-021-01207-y

Wagner, Alan, and Ronald Arkin. 2011. 'Acting deceptively: Providing robots with the capacity for deception', *International Journal of Social Robotics*, 3(1): 5–26, https://doi.org/10.1007/s12369-010-0073-8

Wagner, Alan. 2016. 'Lies and deception: Robots that use falsehood as a social strategy', in *Robots That Talk and Listen: Technology and Social Impact*, ed. by Judith Markowitz (Berlin: de Gruyter), 203–25, https://doi.org/10.1515/9781614514404

Wareham, Christopher. 2021. 'Artificial intelligence and African conceptions of personhood', *Ethics and Information Technology*, 23(2): 127–36, https://doi.org/10.1007/s10676-020-09541-3

Wilks, Yorick. 2010. 'Introducing artificial companions', in *Close Engagements with Artificial Companions*, ed. by Yorick Wilks (Amsterdam: John Benjamins Publishing Co), 11–22. https://doi.org/10.1075/nlp.8

Zhao, Shanyang. 2006. 'Humanoid social robots as a medium of communication', *New Media & Society*, 8(3): 401–19, https://doi.org/10.1177/1461444806061951

4. Climate Engineering and the Future of Justice

Lead authors: *Behnam Taebi, Dominic Lenzi*[1]
Contributing authors: *Lorina Buhr, Kristy Claassen,*
Alessio Gerola, Ben Hofbauer, Elisa Paiusco,
Julia Rijssenbeek

This chapter discusses the societal and ethical challenges of climate engineering or large-scale intentional intervention in the climate system. Climate engineering is highly controversial, and raises many questions about the values of human societies and the desirability of technological visions of the future. Yet existing ethical theories and concepts may not be equipped to deal with the resulting ethical issues. To understand the potential social and political disruptiveness of climate engineering, we argue it must be placed in the context of global environmental changes caused by human activity. However, climate engineering is also accompanied by a high degree of uncertainty and risk in terms of potential and actual unintended impacts on natural processes and society. An important challenge stems from epistemic and normative uncertainties about the reversibility and variability in

---

1   All mentioned lead authors and contributors contributed in some way to this chapter and approved the final version. BT and DL are the lead authors. They coordinated the contributions to this chapter and did the final editing. BT and DL conceptualised and co-wrote the Sections 4.1. and 4.4. DL also co-wrote Section 4.3. and contributed throughout. LB and JR co-wrote Section 4.2., and LB contributed to Section 4.1. EP co-wrote Section 4.3. and contributed to Section 4.2. BH co-wrote Section 4.3. and contributed to Sections 4.1. and 4.2. KC contributed to Section 4.3., and AG contributed to the paper conceptualization and edited several sections.

spatial and temporal scales of deployment. Epistemic uncertainties arise in the methodological framework of climate science, while normative uncertainties arise from the challenge of reconciling a plurality of values. A key question is how forms of climate engineering enforce or hinder disruption in social practices and institutional settings in the direction of a sustainable future. Climate engineering technologies can affect and potentially disrupt existing conceptions of climate and environmental justice, due to the scale and scope of impacts upon people currently living on the planet, future generations, and non-human species and ecosystems. The availability of climate engineering may also require rethinking the responsibility for climate mitigation, as well as applications of the precautionary principle. Climate engineering also raises the question of how the perspectives of affected communities can be adequately represented. While it remains unclear whether climate engineering techniques can genuinely assist in lessening the impacts of climate change, the question is whether and to what extent it should be used as a complementary approach to systemic changes in social, economic, and political practices.

Fig. 4.1 Geoengineering. Credit: Menah Wellen

4.1 Introduction

Technology-driven human activities such as the burning of fossil fuels have propelled the earth into a new geological epoch, the 'Anthropocene', i.e. the era of humankind (Crutzen, 2002). The Anthropocene heralds the prospect of a permanent departure from the benign climate and environmental conditions that were known to our ancestors to a much more dangerous future. Since current activities put us on a pathway towards a 'hothouse Earth' (Steffen et al., 2018), transformative change is necessary. This will doubtless involve highly disruptive interventions directed at the global economy and society.

One set of interventions directed at the climate crisis in particular is known as climate engineering or geoengineering. Climate engineering is defined as 'the deliberate or intentional large-scale intervention in the Earth's climate system, in order to moderate global warming' (Royal Society, 2009: 1). Climate engineering is highly controversial and raises many questions about the values of human societies and the desirability of technological visions of the future. Although human beings have engineered their environment throughout their history (Sandler and Basl, 2013: 1) — think of agriculture, house building, resource extraction — human beings have never previously attempted to engineer the global climate. But this is not due merely to the limits of technology. For earlier civilizations, the very idea that human beings could meaningfully alter 'nature' would have been incomprehensible. Yet since the industrial revolution in the eighteenth century, human activities have unintentionally altered nature on a very large scale. Humans have transformed the earth's soil, water and surface and even the composition of the atmosphere. We can characterize high-modernist interventions into nature as intentional (i.e., deliberate and targeted to human purposes), in contrast to the unintentional but profound impacts of anthropogenic activities upon the global climate and the planet as a whole. Thus, climate engineering may represent the logical end-point to intentional intervention into nature in the Anthropocene. As Corner and Pidgeon noted, 'interference in the global climate is precisely the problem that geoengineering is designed to solve' (Corner and Pidgeon, 2010: 28). Nonetheless, the very idea of large-scale intentional intervention into the global climate seems to run up against the limits of current scientific knowledge and governance capacities. Existing ethical theories and concepts may not be equipped to deal with the resulting ethical issues. The deliberate nature of climate engineering marks these techniques out as ethically distinctive (Jamieson, 1996), and distinguishes them from similar effects produced unintentionally on the Earth's natural systems and processes.[2]

Before discussing these issues, we introduce the two main forms of climate engineering. The climate is regulated by two variables: the incoming energy through solar radiation (i.e., sunlight) and the amount of solar radiation that is retained within the planetary system, mostly through greenhouse gasses (GHG). Climate engineering targets both variables. Solar Radiation Management (SRM) techniques affect the planetary reflection levels, whereas Carbon Dioxide Removal (CDR) techniques remove carbon dioxide from the atmosphere. The forms of climate engineering vary greatly in form, scale, and potential for disruptive impacts (for an assessment of CDR, see IPCC (2022: Chapter 12). For SRM, see IPCC (2018: Chapter 4). Box 1 lists some of the key technologies that are being considered in international climate policy.

---

2   It is more accurate to refer to forms of climate engineering as 'techniques' rather than 'technologies', since many forms of climate engineering do not currently exist or are untested at necessary scale, thus reserving the term 'technology' for functioning socio-technical systems (Rayner, 2010). Another reason for preferring this terminology is that climate engineering includes practices such as reforestation that have been used for millennia, which would be strange to refer to as 'technologies'.

Carbon Dioxide Removal (CDR)

- Afforestation is the planting of forests where no forests have existed previously, while reforestation is the restoration of deforested land.

- Bioenergy with Carbon Capture and Storage (BECCS) features the growth of biomass which removes CO_2 from the air, which is then burned to generate energy. However, carbon capture technology prevents resulting emissions reaching the atmosphere.

- Direct Air Capture with CCS (DACCS) combines CCS with chemical processes to capture CO_2 from ambient air, which is then stored underground.

- Enhanced Weathering (EW) removes atmospheric CO_2 by spreading small particles of ground silicate and carbonate rock onto soils, coasts or oceans.

- Ocean Fertilization (OF) increases the rate at which the ocean draws down atmospheric CO_2 and sequesters it in the deep oceans through the growth of phytoplankton.

Solar Radiation Management (SRM)

- Solar Aerosol Injection (SAI) injects a gas into the atmosphere which then changes into aerosols that block some incoming solar radiation, slightly lowering global average temperature.

- Marine Cloud Brightening (MCB) sprays sea salt or similar particles into marine clouds, increasing their reflectivity and blocking some incoming solar radiation.

- Ground-based Albedo Modification (GBAM) increases the reflectivity of land surfaces, which deflect incoming solar radiation (IPCC 2022).

Box 4.1: An overview of Climate Engineering approaches

Due to the diversity of forms of CDR and SRM, they are generally regarded as raising distinct ethical and governance concerns (Pamplany et al., 2020). In fact, some scholars have argued that grouping two types of fundamentally different techniques into one category is unhelpful and perhaps even misleading (Heyward, 2013; Lenzi, 2018). While both CDR and SRM are controversial, the Royal Society argued that CDR raised fewer ethical concerns. Indeed, some use of CDR is now considered desirable and even necessary to limit warming to 1.5 °C in line with the Paris Agreement. Recent IPCC reports emphasize the goal of 'net zero emissions', which is unattainable without actively removing carbon dioxide (CO_2) from the atmosphere (IPCC, 2022; 2018). SRM techniques and, more specifically, Stratospheric Aerosol Injections (SAI), have provoked the most controversy. Proponents claim it is a feasible technology at a relatively low cost (Keith et al., 2010; Barrett, 2008). However, such estimates ignore indirect costs and impacts. SAI could give rise to large risks (i.e. droughts, effect on agriculture, etc.) in different places from where it is applied, and such risks may manifest in the future rather than at the moment of implementation. This spatial and temporal dispersal of cause and impact has been the subject of significant ethical analysis, as well as trenchant criticisms of its potential for causing injustice (Gardiner, 2010).

With regard to the ethical evaluation of climate engineering, it is worth emphasizing that the levels of intentional intervention and impacts can range from a local to a regional and a planetary scale and from a short-term to long-term intervention. Climate engineering is also accompanied by a high degree of uncertainty and risk in terms of potential and actual unintended impacts on natural processes and society, both spatially and temporally (Corner and Pidgeon, 2010; Sandler and Basl, 2013). In the next section, we review why climate engineering is socially and ecologically disruptive, before moving on to Section 4.3 in which we discuss potential conceptual disruption. In Section 4.4, we will present some directions for the future of philosophy research with respect to climate engineering.

4.2 Impacts and social disruptions

While climate engineering techniques have been proposed with the intended positive physical impacts in mind, they could also give rise to other undesirable and unanticipated impacts. CDR's most obvious intended impact is the reduction of atmospheric CO_2. Because there is a very limited carbon budget remaining for limiting warming to below 1.5 °C, CDR (or 'Negative Emissions Technologies') is regarded by the IPCC as necessary to stabilize the global climate. Nonetheless, there is no requirement to utilize any particular form of CDR, and there is a wide variety of available forms, including 'nature-based' techniques that enhance existing carbon sinks, and engineered carbon removal methods. Clearly, these options raise distinct physical and societal challenges. One prominent technique is Bioenergy with Carbon Capture and Storage, or BECCS, which features heavily in mitigation modeling and in IPCC assessments. A BECCS facility produces energy by burning biomass, with the resulting emissions captured and stored underground or in chemically stable ways, such as through mineralization. This draws down atmospheric CO_2 through the growth of biomass. Ethical concerns with BECCS arise due to the very large scales of envisaged implementation seen in climate mitigation models, which would be necessary in order to have a meaningful impact on the atmospheric concentration of CO_2. Such upscaling would require vast amounts of organic resources including water and arable land, and would compete with other vital land uses such as growing food crops. Clearing land in order to grow BECCS crops could also negatively impact regional biodiversity (Creutzig et al., 2015). Thus, although a single BECCS facility may not have any noteworthy impacts, large-scale implementation would raise concerns about justice and human well-being, especially with regards to vulnerable communities that are likely to be most affected and which may already be disproportionately harmed by climate impacts.

While SRM techniques would block some incoming sunlight, this is not considered to be as a form of climate mitigation or adaptation. Instead, SRM is usually considered as an additional means to reduce some of the most harmful climate change impacts, including rising sea levels and the frequency and severity of extreme weather events (i.e. droughts, floods, hurricanes, etc.). While SRM can be accomplished in a variety of ways, the most commonly discussed approach is through Stratospheric Aerosol Injection, or SAI. This entails spraying aerosols into the stratosphere (10 to 50 kilometers in the atmosphere), increasing the earth's albedo levels. The direct physical impacts are expected to contribute to an overall cooling of the planet, which should practically lead to a reduced rate of global warming, a central driver of catastrophic weather events (Keith, 2013). While model results featuring SAI appear promising in reducing global average temperatures, climate models are simplifications of expected climate system responses and are known to set aside many uncertainties (Pindyck, 2017). This makes reliance upon model results a question of values as well as of epistemic reliability — a point familiar in the philosophy of science as the problem of 'inductive risk' (Rudner, 1953). Put simply, what level of evidence is deemed to be adequate, when the social and ecological consequences of being wrong are severe? In particular, the regional impacts of SAI in such models are highly uncertain and difficult to anticipate because there is very little actual data. This could include impacts on regional weather patterns and climatological forces such as changes in the monsoon, dry and rainy seasons, with obvious implications for food production and biodiversity. Importantly, much of this uncertainty cannot be resolved until the technology is actually deployed (Robock et al., 2008; Kortetmäki and Oksanen, 2016).

For both types of climate engineering, there are several highly problematic ethical implications. These implications are not limited to deployment, but even result from contemplation of some forms of climate engineering, as well as at the research phase. Below, we focus on the potential for social disruption implied by climate engineering. Section 4.3 will address the potential for climate engineering to disrupt conceptions of justice.

As noted at the outset, to understand the potential social and political disruptiveness of climate engineering we must place such interventions in the context of global environmental changes caused by human activity. In conjunction with other drivers of extinction and global environmental change, global warming increases extinction pressures on many species, as ecosystem changes are often too rapid for species to adapt to. The mass extinction of species and the changes in the climate system are two sides of the same coin, caused by resource-intensive, unsustainable fossil-based economies and industrializations (Pimm, 2009). These changes can be understood as socio-ecological disruptions. Faced with socio-ecological disruption of this magnitude, rapid large-scale changes to the global economy and society are required. At the UN Convention on Biological Diversity summit in December 2022, Inger Andersen, Executive Director of UN Environment Programme, pointed to this principal challenge for humanity:

> I invite you to just walk down the street that is yours and ponder what it was a hundred years ago. Everything is converted in many places. So we can't sort of 'push the hot button' and go back to 'what it was-button'. So what we need to understand is that we need to [...] change our way.[3]

To 'change our way' requires disrupting the institutional and technological infrastructures of fossil-based societies, along with ethical norms and values and social practices — it is about 'changing whole systems of economic, technological and social practice' (Urry, 2015: 57).

A key question is how forms of climate engineering enforce or hinder disruption in social practices and institutional settings in the direction of a sustainable future. A number of crucial social, ethical, and political concerns have been raised in relation to climate engineering as a technological response to climate change. First, SRM, and particularly SAI, may be insufficiently disruptive, preventing the much-needed sustainability transformation. In this way, SAI may be more of a 'socially sustaining technology' rather than a 'socially disruptive technology' (Hopster, 2021), but one that does not bring about the necessary societal changes for a sustainable future. As SAI would be deployed temporarily, it can be seen as a means to 'buy time' (Neuber and Ott, 2020) and shave off peak warming scenarios, reducing some of the most severe impacts of climate change. A major concern, however, is that the availability of this technique (even in theory) might disincentivize decarbonization of the global energy system and prolong unjust and unsustainable market and geopolitical arrangements (Schneider and Fuhr, 2020). This effect is the 'moral hazard' (Gardiner, 2010) or 'mitigation obstruction' (Betz and Cacean, 2012), i.e. that the availability of climate engineering could decrease the political commitment to ramp up radical mitigation. This

---

3   This is a quote from an interview with Inger Andersen, Executive Director of UN Environment Programme: https://www.bbc.co.uk/programmes/m001fwh4

straightforwardly applies to forms of SRM such as SAI. Yet it also applies to CDR, because the availability of these techniques affects the stringency of mitigation by shifting some near-term mitigation to the future within scenario research (Lenzi, 2018). A related issue is whether CDR leaves the door open for the continuation of the fossil economy, including its existing power structures and dominant agents. Many of the actors best placed to take advantage of CDR (due to existing infrastructure and ownership of appropriate sites) are also leading historical contributors to climate change, including fossil fuel companies. While these companies continue to actively lobby against climate policy, they appear to be repositioning themselves as 'carbon removal' businesses. Historical track records of these giant fossil companies contribute to these worries. For example, privately funded research by Exxon Mobil in 1970 accurately predicted global temperature rise the world is currently experiencing (Cuff, 2023). Given that such companies have a record of putting private profits ahead of the public good (Oreskes and Conway, 2010), the implementation of CDR by such actors may similarly entrench private interests above the global interest in stringent climate mitigation.

Research on some forms of climate engineering could also be highly politically disruptive, raising the need for appropriate governance frameworks. An individual country or even wealthy individual actor could unilaterally decide to carry out research or even deploy SAI (Preston, 2013). For this reason, some argue that there is an urgent need to establish research governance structures to ensure equitable decision-making (NASEM, 2021; McLaren and Corry, 2021; Wagner, 2021). While CDR also poses institutional and governance challenges, many of these arise in the context of climate mitigation and sustainable development. Governing the implications of CDR requires consideration of potential effects upon the stringency of mitigation itself, along with effects of CDR deployment upon other priorities in the context of the Sustainable Development Goals, notably the alleviation of poverty and the prevention of transboundary environmental harm between sovereign states (Honegger et al., 2022). The sourcing of sustainable biomass will be a particular challenge for BECCS. A pure market approach based upon lowest cost would likely mean biomass being grown primarily in the Global South, leading to acute worries about food security and biodiversity impacts (Anderson and Peters, 2016). This is similar to the introduction of biofuel in the first decade of this century that led to a global food crisis, particularly in the Global South (Taebi, 2021: Chapter 6). A new rush for biofuels could allow for the exploitation of biomass producers in the Global South. The differences between SRM and CDR also imply differences for desirable or appropriate governance. Particularly because SRM would immediately have a global effect on the climate, as well as regional (weather) effects, politically legitimate international governance structures will need to account for the spatial and temporal dispersal of impacts (Szerszynski et al., 2013; Heyward and Rayner, 2013; Gardiner and Fragnière, 2016). For CDR, participatory governance regimes are needed regarding the siting location of carbon removal facilities (Honegger et al., 2022).

4.3 Conceptual disruption

Climate engineering technologies can affect and potentially disrupt existing conceptions of climate and environmental justice. This is due to the scale and scope of impacts, which includes wealthy and poor individuals currently alive on Earth, unborn future generations, non-human species, and ecosystems. Of course, climate change itself, along with climate mitigation and adaptation policies, have or will have such impacts. Thus, attention to distributive justice has long been a feature of climate ethics; in particular the question of what would constitute a fair distribution of the burdens of climate policy (Gardiner et al., 2010). Appeals to justice are also a feature of international climate negotiations. Developing nations and small island states have insisted that wealthy industrialized nations take the lead in cutting their emissions and funding the adaptation of nations least historically responsible, while wealthy nations have resisted such calls.[4]

While justice has long been a feature of climate discourses, the additional impacts of climate engineering — both beneficial and harmful — cast these issues of justice in a new light. The availability of climate engineering, both in terms of CDR and SRM, may require a rethinking of some dimensions of climate justice, such as the contents

---

4   The UNFCCC principle of 'common but differentiated responsibilities' reflects the place of distributive justice in climate politics but does little to mitigate disagreements, since the principle is vague and does not create binding obligations upon parties.

of a responsibility to mitigate. We are the first humans to understand the essential dynamics of the planet's climate, as well as humanity's combined influence upon it. As Shue (2021) has recently argued, this unique historical context makes the current generation a pivotal generation with unprecedented moral responsibility to mitigate climate change. This responsibility connects with some forms of climate engineering in an obvious way, especially as the IPCC has recently reclassified CDR as 'mitigation' rather than climate 'engineering' (IPCC, 2022: Chapter 12). As noted in Section 4.1, because too little mitigation has happened, it is very likely that limiting warming to 'well below 2 °C' will require the use of CDR. However, it remains unclear exactly what would constitute an intergenerationally fair distribution of the burdens of CDR across existing and future generations. As noted in Section 4.2, the example of BECCS shows this clearly: an ungoverned expansion in the global demand for biomass could undermine basic needs by increasing food prices and water scarcity, harm biodiversity, and incentivize land-grabbing in the name of carbon storage. CDR also introduces a potential trade-off between (spatial) social justice and intergenerational social justice. Authors have noted that CDR would extend the global carbon budget, thereby allowing for a longer period of fossil-fuelled development in the Global South to alleviate extreme poverty (Morrow and Svoboda, 2016; Moellendorf, 2022). Thus, the availability of CDR affects how we might think about the obligations of countries, and global obligations of distributive justice in relation to climate change. The current generation therefore faces two options: more ambitious mitigation now via large emissions cuts coupled with relatively small CDR reliance, or less ambitious mitigation to allow for further economic development coupled with the assumption future people will be able to recover from an overshoot through very large-scale CDR.

Because the availability of CDR affects country mitigation policies, and has the potential to shift some decarbonization to the future, another implication is the risk of policy failure to achieve such emission cuts in the future. Therefore, a prevalent concern in the literature is that plans to massively scale up CDR represent a high-stakes gamble on unproven technologies (Fuss et al., 2014; Anderson and Peters, 2016). The ethical literature has examined the implications of such a gamble for intergenerational ethics (Shue, 2017; 2018; Lenzi, 2021). According to Shue (2017; 2018), such a gamble on CDR would be especially problematic insofar as future people cannot consent to making it, but would be the ones affected should the gamble fail.

It is even more controversial whether a responsibility to urgently mitigate or adapt to climate change includes a responsibility to research and ultimately deploy SRM. The ethical and governance literature is highly polarized on this point. Indeed, an influential group of scientists has recently published a SRM 'non-use agreement' calling for a boycott of research, citing concerns with governance and justice (Biermann et al., 2022). For SRM, justice concerns with SAI in particular highlight the potential for unequally distributed negative impacts. As Preston (2013) notes, a world artificially cooled by SAI raises questions about whose interests ought to be protected, and it is far from clear that the interests of the most vulnerable would be prioritized if SAI were ever implemented, or that fair compensation would be given to those subjected to additional harms. Even if we assume that SAI slightly lowered global average temperatures and thus avoided some of the harmful global impacts of climate change (such as sea level rise), the side-effects of SAI may create additional harmful impacts such as affecting precipitation patterns, including the Indian monsoon (Robock et al., 2008). By potentially exacerbating severe weather impact, SAI has the potential to impose severe injustice upon people who have the least ability to adapt.

The potential for SAI to rapidly reduce some of the impacts of climate change also complicates the question of what countries owe one another or to future generations. As noted earlier, this possibility has been framed as a way of 'buying time' for mitigation (Neuber and Ott, 2020; Betz and Cacean, 2012). Some advocates of SRM research have long claimed that, facing insufficient mitigation, there is a moral responsibility to deploy SRM to protect human rights (Horton and Keith, 2016). But many oppose this kind of argument (Gardiner, 2010; McKinnon, 2020; McLaren, 2016; Flegal and Gupta, 2017). Hourdequin (2018) claims that this overly narrow view of justice that presents SRM at the core of its approach ignores the distribution of epistemic power and power to make decisions about climate policy, and hence questions of procedural and recognition justice bearing upon SRM research. Some advocates similarly point to SAI as a means to avoid the greater injustice of runaway climate change, thus framing it as a 'lesser evil'. However, Gardiner (2010) has forcefully objected to framing SAI in this way, arguing that any plan to utilize SAI would be predicated upon the moral failure of the current generation to mitigate its emissions. It has also been argued that pursuing SRM would actually abdicate the moral responsibilities to resolve the root cause of climate change, in favor of a risky 'technofix' (Hamilton, 2013; Biermann et al., 2022). Nonetheless, the continued growth of global emissions and the very tight timeline for limiting warming to below 1.5 °C implies that the importance of these questions will intensify.

Climate engineering also implies rethinking some ideas of moral, and also potential legal responsibility for side-effects resulting from implementation. While climate change was unintentionally brought about as a side-effect of other activities, at least some climate engineering activities (most obviously SAI) directly aim to alter global warming, and we have some foresight concerning potential side-effects. The moral responsibility attributed to such harms turns upon showing that an actor intentionally sought to manipulate the climate system, and whether they knew or should have known about potential side-effects of their action.[5] However, not all side-effects are knowable in advance. For SAI, some side-effects are unknowable prior to implementation. Even for CDR, while there are already known side-effects of large-scale CDR implementation, particularly for land-based techniques such as BECCS, these effects are jointly produced by millions of actors in complex causal chains that can span the whole globe, such as food production and exports. Very large-scale afforestation and reforestation projects would also affect regional and global precipitation patterns (Scharping, 2022). Such possibilities may leave the moral responsibilities for CDR side-effects underdetermined, similarly with the debate about individual climate responsibilities (Nefsky, 2019). Legal responsibilities may come apart from moral responsibilities if there are existing institutional obligations in place, such as the obligation upon states to avoid causing transboundary environmental harm, which applies independently

---

5   This is why evidence that fossil fuel companies knew or had reasonably justified beliefs that their actions contributed to climate change, and that this was dangerously absent from their policy responses, is a basis for holding them morally and potentially legally responsible. This is despite the fact that the intention of fossil fuel companies was to make money rather than to cause climate change for its own sake. In this context, the prioritization of profits at the expense of the public interest in climate policy and the deliberate production of climate misinformation adds substantially to such responsibility.

of the attribution of an intention to cause harm. Similarly, there is a link with the *Precautionary Principle*, or the principle that argues that lack of full scientific knowledge about a potential risk is insufficient reason to assume that there is no risk; sometimes we should refrain from action if the nature or the magnitude of the known consequences are unacceptable.[6] The mandated applications of the precautionary principle — to the effect that we might consider refraining from action by states, such as within the European Union, — may imply legal responsibilities for states implementing certain forms of climate engineering to act in accordance with precautionary norms, whether or not harm is intended.

Relatedly, questions of how to compensate for damage caused by climate change internationally will be increasingly difficult after large-scale applications of climate engineering are deployed. In the Conference of Parties gathering in Sharm El Sheikh (COP27) in November 2022, countries for the first time agreed to establish a Loss and Damage fund for the purpose of supporting countries most in need (and historically least responsible for causing the damage) to remediate some climate harms. While it is not clear yet how loss and damage will be determined, causality will likely play an important role. Climate engineering makes the already extremely complex climate systems even more complicated, which will further complicate the attribution of responsibilities to parties.

A further area where climate engineering seems to recast existing notions concerns procedural justice. Many forms of climate engineering also raise difficult challenges regarding procedural justice, given the very wide set of potentially affected parties, which may include the global population, future generations, and even non-human nature. Preston (2013) notes that procedural justice is one of the biggest ethical challenges posed by climate engineering. This conclusion appears most plausible for some forms of SRM. For SAI in particular, procedural justice raises particular challenges even at the research and development stage. Indeed, Preston (2013) concludes that procedural justice is unlikely to be satisfied for SAI, given that any implementation of this technique would immediately affect every person living at the time, and all future generations until SAI ceased. Thus, 'the prospect of controlling the global

---

6   The Rio Declaration on Environment and Development. See Section 4.4. for discussions on the Precautionary Principle.

thermostat is something that all citizens could reasonably claim to have a legitimate stake in' (Corner and Pidgeon, 2010). Such difficulties have encouraged returning to existing legal frameworks that could be brought to bear upon SAI, such as the ENMOD Convention, which is a Cold War arms control treaty that applies to technologies that modify the environment (McGee et al., 2021). While it has been argued that SAI is not necessarily incompatible with democracy or with robust democratic governance (Horton et al., 2018), there seems to be no compelling reason to expect the governance of SAI to actually be democratic. These procedural concerns are conditioned by the mismatch between vulnerability and responsibility for climate change, exacerbated by the fact that developed countries have more political power and are more capable of representing their interests, whereas the less developed are unfavorably placed to call them to account (Gardiner, 2010: 286). Indeed, a major procedural challenge is the expert-analytic character of the geoengineering debate — both for SRM and CDR — and the limited engagement of stakeholders. This is exacerbated by the lack of awareness of the Southern public, primarily in Afro-Asian countries (Pamplany et al., 2020: 3105). Climate engineering raises the question of how the perspectives of communities, specifically those poised to be disproportionately affected by these interventions, can be adequately represented.

The question becomes all the more vexing when considering the risks of further entrenching the discourse along colonial lines. Incorporating intercultural perspectives would thus have to reach beyond the tendency of non-Indigenous researchers to instrumentalize Indigenous communities for or against a particular argument concerning climate engineering (Whyte, 2012; 2017). The multiplicity of Indigenous ontologies, epistemologies, and ethical systems calls for nuanced stakeholder engagement in local contexts. Such engagement allows for redefining concepts such as agency or justice that suits the contexts in which climate engineering technologies will be researched and deployed. For example, the aforementioned issue of intergenerational justice takes a position of prominence in Ubuntu practicing communities as these communities typically conceive of the social community in much broader terms than traditionally Western conceptualizations. The living generation is understood to have duties and obligations towards previous and coming generations. Wiredu (1994: 46) illustrates this when noting that within African Indigenous communities, no duty is as imperious as the husbanding of resources for posterity and that 'in this moral scheme the rights of the unborn play such a cardinal role that any traditional African would be nonplussed by the debate in Western philosophy as to the existence of such rights'. In climate engineering interventions, the duty towards coming generations would thus be framed more centrally than in some non-African communities. There are an abundance of examples illustrating how Indigenous thought can shape, challenge, and critique the dominant discourse. Intercultural perspectives are needed both to account for the variety of viewpoints at stake in climate engineering and to formulate richer ethical accounts of the impacts of climate engineering on wellbeing, social, and political life, and on human relations with non-humans and with the environment (Lazrus et al., 2022).

4.4 Looking ahead

A fundamental challenge for the ethical and political assessment of climate engineering are the underlying, often irreducible uncertainties about the reversibility and variability in spatial and temporal scales of climate engineering deployment. Knowledge about climate change and biodiversity loss is characterized by epistemic uncertainty in terms of variables and databases, but also by 'deep uncertainty' due to the overall framework of model-based knowledge production (Marchau et al., 2019). These uncertainties challenge our empirical and epistemic grasp of the impacts of climate engineering. But climate engineering also raises normative uncertainties (Taebi et al., 2020). These normative uncertainties can best be understood as uncertainties that arise due to a plurality of values which need to be reconciled on a spatiotemporal scale. This entails accounting for different, often opposing, regional, cultural, and individual values as well as the values of future generations. Normative uncertainties could also arise as a result of evolving technologies or evolving moral norms (and values) in the future, which could pose new and unanticipated ethical challenges; this is referred to as techno-moral change (Swierstra et al., 2009) and it is very relevant for contemplating the future of climate engineering technologies (Hofbauer, 2022). An inherent source of epistemic uncertainty is the methodological framework of climate science. Knowledge about climate change is mostly produced by data-intensive models, which are by definition incomplete representations of the real world, but which may also lack important variables that are (as yet) understudied or lacking adequate data. For example, scientists have limited data on the volume and effects of methane gas which is being emitted from the thawing of the Siberian permafrost. Methane is a greenhouse gas, 25 times more potent than carbon dioxide. One way of dealing with these uncertainties is by ensuring that the implementation of either research or deployment proposals for climate engineering technologies do not lead to lock-in or 'slippery slope' situations. In other words, policy plans exploring climate engineering as part of a climate action portfolio should ensure that any implementation remains reversible or as reversible as realistically possible.

However, now that there is a state of scientific consensus on the magnitude and severity of disruptions due to human-induced global warming, lack of data or epistemic uncertainty should not be used as an excuse for not acting against the potentially irreversible harm caused by climate change. A legal and political tool to deal with the problem of irreversibility and risk is to base international political action and shared decision-making upon formulations of the precautionary principle targeted at irreversible or catastrophic environmental and climate harms (Sunstein, 2010; Hartzell-Nichols, 2012). The 1992 Rio Declaration already contains a version of this principle: 'Where there are threats of serious or irreversible damage, lack of full scientific certainty shall not be used as a reason for postponing cost-effective measures to prevent environment degradation' (Principle 15 of the Rio Declaration on Environment and Development). Taking the precautionary principle seriously at local, national and international levels requires a shift in values and an overall assessment of irreversible climate change and biodiversity loss and damage: irreversible loss and damage are difficult to pay for. The emphasis and effort should be on precautionary policies. Thus, it seems challenging to interpret whether climate engineering techniques meet the requirements of acting under the precautionary principle.

A related issue is the feasibility of climate engineering proposals. Although the concept of feasibility is vague and difficult to assess, implicit judgements about whether climate engineering proposals are politically or economically feasible abound in both scientific and ethical literature. Most notably, the IPCC included an assessment of climate policy feasibility (including CDR) in its Special Report, and again in its Sixth Assessment Report (IPCC, 2018; 2022). However, there remain serious epistemic as well as normative problems in attempting to assess feasibility, especially political feasibility. Critics have pointed out that the IPCC ignored the role of equity and justice considerations and the limited expertise of climate scientists in assessing political proposals (Lenzi and Kowarsch, 2021). Extra caution is required since claims about what is economically or politically infeasible can be disguised as statements of willingness, knowledge or even strategic attempts to secure advantage (Schuppert and Seidel, 2017).

More fundamentally, climate engineering raises questions about the values of climate policy and the desirability of purely technological solutions. To Paul Crutzen, who coined the term 'Anthropocene', humanity had to move from unintentional environmental modification to embrace a responsibility to intentionally manage (or 'optimize', as he put it) the global climate in 'our' own interests (Crutzen, 2002: 23). The technocratic perspective implied is problematic for several reasons. First, several commentators have argued that trying to 'fix' the climate through climate engineering techniques is tantamount to Western technological hubris (Jamieson, 1996). SRM in the form of SAI in particular seems to reflect a hubristic vision of humanity controlling the climate, thereby affecting planetary conditions (Hamilton, 2013; Hulme, 2014; 2017). For CDR, a similar concern arises in relation to very large-scale implementation scenarios found in some climate models, which would effectively mean human beings collectively managing the global carbon cycle, despite our lack of understanding of many relevant planetary feedbacks and indirect effects (Lenzi, 2018). It is also unclear whose interests should matter. Many leading climate ethicists have argued that climate change should be responded to in a way that protects the human rights or basic needs of current and future generations (Caney, 2010; Cripps, 2013; Shue, 1993; 2019). However, as we saw in the previous section, in the context of climate engineering research and potential implementation there are serious doubts about whether the human rights or basic needs of all will be protected. For instance, some have worried that any deployment of SRM would serve the interests of a 'geoclique' of the wealthy and powerful (McKinnon, 2020), while others believe this deployment could be both inclusive and fairly shared (Morrow, 2020). A further key issue is whether the interests of non-humans should count in any consideration of climate engineering. The technocratic assumption of managing the global climate in the interests of human beings is silent on whether this would include consideration of non-humans for their own sake in the manner of ecological trusteeship, or would merely involve an instrumental form of natural resource stewardship. A general weakness of ethical literature on climate engineering, as with climate ethics more broadly (McShane, 2016), is its lack of engagement with environmental ethics arguments concerning the moral significance of non-human interests (e.g. Rolston III, 1988). This point raises interesting possibilities for future research. In considering the impact of climate change upon the future of non-human species and ecosystems, it seems essential to reconsider the ethical impacts of climate change in non-anthropocentric terms (Nolt, 2011; McShane, 2016). Nolt (2015) extends this argument to also refer to important technological interventions with potentially significant environmental impact such as nuclear energy production. At present, there is very little research on the implications of climate engineering for non-humans, or what environmental values research generally implies for climate engineering. Similarly, it is important to explore the impacts of different climate engineering techniques in non-anthropocentric terms.

Future research on climate engineering may also engage with analyses of the meaning of 'nature' in the Anthropocene (Latour, 2017). As Preston (2012) explains, although the claim that climate change implied the 'end of nature' often operates with a philosophically oversimplified notion of 'nature', it might nonetheless be insightful in relation to climate engineering. According to Preston, the prospect of climate engineering relates to the 'end of nature', because intentional modification of the global climate would create an artificial rather than natural planet. Preston identified two more precise narratives of 'artificing' the planet: first, that climate engineering could be viewed as a planetary attempt at ecological restoration, where although human intentions are part of the functioning of the climate system, the Earth does not become 'a giant artifact' (Preston, 2012: 194) because much space for wildness and unexpectedness remains in the functioning of natural processes, and second that artificing concerns the implications of a planetary expansion of responsibility for managing the climate, in line with Crutzen's (2002) view. Preston notes that

SRM thrusts us into the role of designer and caretaker of both people and ecosystems. We must manage the climate to be both maximally restorative and minimally risky. We must do this at a global scale in the face of considerable — and perhaps ineliminable — uncertainty in the sciences. This is clearly a daunting challenge. (2012: 197)

Nonetheless, as Preston also notes, the long-standing critiques of the concept of 'nature' in environmental philosophy would caution against any straightforward inferences concerning the naturalness or artificiality of climate engineering. One of the more notable is Plumwood's (1993) ecofeminist critique against the identification of the natural with the feminine and the unruly, which needed to be subdued or dominated by masculine notions of control. Recent contributors have even called for dispensing with the concept of nature entirely in view of its loss of meaning (Vogel, 2015), or rethinking it fundamentally by purging it of the problematic dualism of nature/culture (Latour, 2017). Further engagement with 'nature' in relation to climate engineering would require exploration of the intercultural dimensions of nature and environmental values. There is a wide diversity of traditions on environmental ethics with various uses for the concept (or none), including Asian traditions (Callicott and McRae, 2014) and Indigenous and local traditions (Callicott, 1994). Further, the recent assessment conducted by the Intergovernmental Science-Policy Platform on Biodiversity and Ecosystem Services (IPBES, 2022) found a high diversity of environmental values and worldviews across the world, again including some that do not recognise any concept of 'nature'. Given the existence of multiple and conflicting understandings of nature, there does not seem to be any straightforward way to assess the implications of climate engineering.

It remains unclear whether climate engineering techniques can genuinely assist in lessening the impacts of climate change, or assist societies in moving from the fossil-based technologies and land-degrading practices that have brought the Earth into the Anthropocene. From an ethical and political perspective, the question is whether and to what extent climate engineering can and should be used as a complementary approach to systemic changes in social, economic and political practices. Nonetheless, it is clear that the question of how to appropriately govern climate engineering research and deployment requires establishing effective inter- and transnational institutions that address these issues of global responsibility, inequality, uncertainty, and potential sources of new injustices between deploying actors (e.g. national actors) and the interests of those affected.

Further listening and watching

Readers who would like to learn more about the topics discussed in this chapter might be interested in listening to these episodes of the ESDiT podcast (https://anchor.fm/esdit) and other videos:

Behnam Taebi on 'Climate risks and normative uncertainties': https://podcasters.spotify.com/pod/show/esdit/episodes/Behnam-Taebi-on-Climate-Risk-and-Normative-Uncertainties-e1gc7o8/a-a7lfbdv

Ben Hofbauer on 'Geo-engineering and techno-moral change': https://podcasters.spotify.com/pod/show/esdit/episodes/Ben-Hofbauer-on-Geo-engineering--techno-moral-change-e1k1oae/a-a84c4fd

References

Anderson, Kevin, and Glen Peters. 2016. 'The trouble with negative emissions', *Science*, 354(6309): 182–83, https://doi.org/10.1126/science.aah4567

Barrett, Scott. 2008. 'The incredible economics of geoengineering', *Environmental & Resource Economics*, 39: 45–54, https://doi.org/10.1007/s10640-007-9174-8

Betz, Gregor, and Sebastian Cacean. 2012. *Ethical Aspects of Climate Engineering* (Karlsruhe: Karlsruhe Institut für Technologie)

Biermann, Frank, Jeroen Oomen, Aarti Gupta, Saleem H. Ali, Ken Conca, Maarten A. Hajer, Prakash Kashwan, Louis J. Kotzé, Melissa Leach, Dirk Messner, Chukwumerije Okereke, Åsa Persson, Janez Potočnik, David Schlosberg, Michelle Scobie, and Stacy D. VanDeveer. 2022. 'Solar geoengineering: The case for an international non-use agreement', *WIREs Climate Change*, 13(3): e754, https://doi.org/10.1002/wcc.754

Callicott, J. Baird. 1994. *Earth's Insights. A Survey of Ecological Ethics from the Mediterranean Basin to the Australian Outback* (Berkeley, LA; London, UK: University of California Press).

Callicott, J. Baird, and James McRae (eds). 2014. *Environmental Philosophy in Asian Traditions of Thought* (New York: State University of New York Press)

Caney, Simon. 2010. 'Climate change, human rights, and moral thresholds', in *Climate Ethics: Essential Readings*, ed. by Stephen M. Gardiner, Simon Caney, Dale Jamieson, and Henry Shue (Oxford: Oxford University Press), 163–77.

Corner, Adam, and Nick Pidgeon. 2010. 'Geoengineering the climate: The social and ethical implications', *Environment: Science and Policy for Sustainable Development*, 52(1): 24–37, https://doi.org/10.1080/00139150903479563

Creutzig, Felix, N. H. Ravindranath, Göran Berndes, Simon Bolwig, Ryan Bright, Francesco Cherubini, Helena Chum, Esteve Corbera, Mark Delucchi, Andre Faaij, Joseph Fargione, Helmut Haberl, Garvin Heath, Oswaldo Lucon, Richard Plevin, Alexander Popp, Carmenza Robledo-Abad, Steven Rose, Pete Smith, Anders Stromman, Sangwon Suh, and Omar Masera. 2015. 'Bioenergy and climate change mitigation: An assessment', *GCB Bioenergy*, 7(5): 916–44, https://doi.org/10.1111/gcbb.12205

Cripps, Elizabeth. 2013. *Climate Change and the Moral Agent: Individual Duties in an Interdependent World* (Oxford: Oxford University Press)

Crutzen, Paul J. 2002. 'Geology of mankind', *Nature*, 415: 23, https://doi.org/10.1038/415023a

Cuff, Madeleine. 2023. 'Exxon scientists in the 1970s accurately predicted climate change', *New Scientist*, https://www.newscientist.com/article/2354492-exxon-scientists-in-the-1970s-accurately-predicted-climate-change/

Flegal, Jane A., and Aarti Gupta. 2017. 'Evoking equity as a rationale for solar geoengineering research? Scrutinizing emerging expert visions of equity', *International Environmental Agreements: Politics, Law and Economics*, 18: 45–61, https://doi.org/10.1007/s10784-017-9377-6

Fuss, Sabine, Josep G. Canadell, Glen P. Peters, Massimo Tavoni, Robbie M. Andrew, Philippe Ciais, Robert B. Jackson, Chris D. Jones, Florian Kraxner, Nebosja Nakicenovic, Corinne Le Quéré, Michael R. Raupach, Ayyoob Sharifi, Pete Smith, and Yoshiki Yamagata. 2014. 'Betting on negative emissions', *Nature Climate Change*, 4(10): 850–53, https://doi.org/10.1038/nclimate2392

Gardiner, Stephen. 2010. 'Is "arming the future" with geoengineering really the lesser evil?', in *Climate Ethics: Essential Readings*, ed. by Stephen M. Gardiner, Simon Caney, Dale Jamieson, and Henry Shue (Oxford: Oxford University Press), 284–312

Gardiner, Stephen, Simon Caney, Dale Jamieson, and Henry Shue (eds). 2010. *Climate Ethics: Essential Readings* (Oxford: Oxford University Press)

Gardiner, Stephen, and Augustin Fragnière. 2016. 'Why geoengineering is not Plan B', in *Climate Justice and Geoengineering*, ed. by Christopher J. Preston (London: Rowman & Littlefield), 15–32.

Hamilton, Clive. 2013. *Earthmasters: The Dawn of the Age of Climate Engineering* (New Haven; London: Yale University Press)

Hartzell-Nichols, Lauren. 2012. 'How is climate change harmful?', *Ethics and the Environment*, 17(2): 97–110, https://doi.org/10.2979/ethicsenviro.17.2.97

Heyward, Clare. 2013. 'Situating and abandoning geoengineering: A typology of five responses to dangerous climate change', *PS: Political Science & Politics*, 46 (1): 23–27, https://doi.org/10.1017/S1049096512001436

Heyward, Clare, and Steve Rayner. 2013. 'A curious asymmetry: Social science expertise and geoengineering', *Climate Geoengineering Governance Working Paper Series: 007*, https://www.academia.edu/download/32517700/workingpaper7heywardrayneracuriousasymmetry.pdf

Hofbauer, Benjamin. 2022. 'Techno-moral change through solar geoengineering: How geoengineering challenges sustainability', *Prometheus*, 38(1): 82–97, https://doi.org/10.13169/prometheus.38.1.0082

Honegger, Matthias, Christian Baatz, Samuel Eberenz, Antonia Holland-Cunz, Axel Michaelowa, Benno Pokorny, Matthias Poralla, and Malte Winkler. 2022. 'The ABC of governance principles for carbon dioxide removal policy', *Frontiers in Climate*, 4: 884163, https://doi.org/10.3389/fclim.2022.884163

Hopster, Jeroen. 2021. 'What are socially disruptive technologies?', *Technology in Society*, 67: 101750, https://doi.org/10.1016/j.techsoc.2021.101750

Horton, Joshua, and David Keith. 2016. 'Solar geoengineering and obligations to the global poor', in *Climate Justice and Geoengineering. Ethics and Policy in the Atmospheric Anthropocene*, ed. by Christopher J. Preston (London; New York: Rowman & Littlefield), 79–92.

Horton, Joshua, Jesse Reynolds, Holly Jean Buck, Daniel Callies, Stefan Schäfer, David Keith, and Steve Rayner. 2018. 'Solar geoengineering and democracy', *Global Environmental Politics*, 18(3): 5–24, https://doi.org/10.1162/glep_a_00466

Hourdequin, Marion. 2018. 'Climate change, climate engineering, and the "global poor": What does justice require?', *Ethics, Policy & Environment*, 21(3): 270–88, https://doi.org/10.1080/21550085.2018.1562525

Hulme, Mike. 2014. *Can Science Fix Climate Change? A Case Against Climate Engineering* (Cambridge: Polity Press)

——. 2017. 'Calculating the incalculable: Is SAI the lesser of two evils?', *Ethics & International Affairs*, 31(4): 507–12, https://doi.org/10.1017/S0892679417000491

IPBES. 2022. 'Summary for policymakers of the methodological assessment of the diverse values and valuation of nature of the Intergovernmental Science-Policy Platform on Biodiversity and Ecosystem Services (IPBES)', *IPBES Secretariat*, https://doi.org/10.5281/zenodo.6522392

IPCC. 2018. *Global Warming of 1.5°C. An IPCC Special Report on the Impacts of Global Warming of 1.5°C above Pre-Industrial Levels and Related Global Greenhouse Gas Emission Pathways, in the Context of Strengthening the Global Response to the Threat of Climate Change, Sustainable Development, and Efforts to Eradicate Poverty* (Geneva: World Meteorological Organization), https://www.ipcc.ch/sr15/

———. 2022. *Climate Change 2022: Mitigation of Climate Change.* Contribution of Working Group III to the Sixth Assessment Report of the Intergovernmental Panel on Climate Change (Cambridge: Cambridge University Press), https://www.ipcc.ch/report/sixth-assessment-report-working-group-3/

Jamieson, Dale. 1996. 'Ethics and intentional climate change', *Climatic Change,* 33: 323–36, https://doi.org/10.1007/BF00142580

Keith, David W., Edward Parson, and M. Granger Morgan. 2010. 'Research on global sun block needed now', *Nature,* 463 (7280): 426–27, https://doi.org/10.1038/463426a

Kortetmäki, Teea, and Markuu Oksanen. 2016. 'Food systems and climate engineering: A plate full of risks or promises?', in *Climate Justice and Geoengineering: Ethics and Policy in the Atmospheric Anthropocene,* ed. by Christopher J. Preston (London: Rowman & Littlefield), 121–36

Latour, Bruno. 2017. *Facing Gaia: Eight Lectures on the New Climatic Regime* (Cambridge: Polity Press)

Lazrus, Heather, Julie Maldonado, Paulette Blanchard, M. Kalani Souza, Bill Thomas, and Danial Wildcat. 2022. 'Culture change to address climate change: Collaborations with Indigenous and Earth sciences for more just, equitable, and sustainable responses to our climate crisis', *PLoS Climate,* 1(2): e0000005, https://doi.org/10.1371/journal.pclm.0000005

Lenzi, Dominic. 2018. 'The ethics of negative emissions', *Global Sustainability,* 1(e7): 1–8, https://doi.org/10.1017/sus.2018.5

———. 2021. 'On the permissibility (or otherwise) of negative emissions', *Ethics, Policy & Environment,* 24(2): 123–36, https://doi.org/10.1080/21550085.2021.1885249

Lenzi, Dominic, and Martin Kowarsch. 2021. 'Integrating justice in climate policy assessments: Towards a deliberative transformation of feasibility', in *Climate Justice and Political Feasibility,* ed. by Sarah Kenehan and Corey Katz (London: Rowman and Littlefield)

Marchau, Vincent, Warren Walker, Pieter Bloemen, and Steven Popper (eds). 2019. *Decision Making Under Deep Uncertainty: From Theory to Practice* (Cham: Springer), https://doi.org/10.1007/978-3-030-05252-2

McGee, Jeffrey, Kerryn Brent, Jan McDonald, and Clare Heyward. 2021. 'International governance of solar radiation management: Does the ENMOD Convention deserve a closer look?', *Carbon & Climate Law Review,* 14(4): 294–305, https://doi.org/10.21552/cclr/2020/4/8

McKinnon, Catriona. 2020. 'The Panglossian politics of the geoclique', *Critical Review of International Social and Political Philosophy*, 23(5): 584–99, https://doi.org/10.1080/13698230.2020.1694216

McLaren, Duncan. 2016. 'Framing out justice: The post-politics of climate engineering discourses', in *Climate Justice and Geoengineering: Ethics and Policy in the Atmospheric Anthopocene*, ed. by Christopher J. Preston (London: Rowman and Littlefield)

McLaren, Duncan, and Olaf Corry. 2021. 'The politics and governance of research into solar geoengineering', *WIREs Climate Change*, 12(3): 1–20, https://doi.org/10.1002/wcc.707

McShane, Katie. 2016. 'Anthropocentrism in climate ethics and climate policy', *Midwest Studies in Philosophy*, 40(1): 189–204, https://doi.org/10.1111/misp.12055

Moellendorf, Darrel. 2022. *Mobilizing Hope: Climate Change & Global Poverty* (Oxford; New York: Oxford University Press).

Morrow, David. 2020. 'A mission-driven research program on solar geoengineering could promote justice and legitimacy', *Critical Review of International Social and Political Philosophy*, 23(5): 618–40, https://doi.org/10.1080/13698230.2020.1694220

Morrow, David, and Toby Svoboda. 2016. 'Geoengineering and non-ideal theory', *Public Affairs Quarterly*, 30(1): 83–102.

NASEM. 2021. *Reflecting Sunlight: Recommendations for Solar Geoengineering Research and Research Governance* (Washington DC: The National Academies Press), https://doi.org/10.17226/25762

Nefsky, Julia. 2019. 'Collective harm and the inefficacy problem', *Philosophy Compass*, 14(4): e12587. https://doi.org/10.1111/phc3.12587

Neuber, Frederike, and Konrad Ott. 2020. 'The buying time argument within the solar radiation management discourse', *Applied Sciences*, 10(13): 4637, https://doi.org/10.3390/app10134637

Nolt, John. 2011. 'Nonanthropocentric climate ethics', *WIREs Climate Change*, 2(5): 701–11, https://doi.org/10.1002/wcc.131

——. 2015. 'Non-Anthropocentric nuclear energy ethics', in *The Ethics of Nuclear Energy: Risk, Justice and Democracy in the Post-Fukushima Era*, ed. by Behnam Taebi and Sabine Roeser (Cambridge: Cambridge University Press), 157–75

Oreskes, Naomi, and Erik M. Conway. 2010. *Merchants of Doubt: How a Handful of Scientists Obscured the Truth on Issues from Tobacco Smoke to Global Warming* (New York: Bloomsbury Press)

Pamplany, Augustine, Bert Gordijn, and Patrick Brereton. 2020. 'The ethics of geoengineering: A literature review', *Science and Engineering Ethics*, 26(6): 3069–119, https://doi.org/10.1007/s11948-020-00258-6

Pimm, Stuart. 2009. 'Climate disruption and biodiversity', *Current Biology*, 19(14): R595–601. https://doi.org/10.1016/j.cub.2009.05.055

Pindyck, Robert. 2017. 'The use and misuse of models for climate policy', *Review of Environmental Economics and Policy*, 11(1): 100–14, https://doi.org/10.1093/reep/rew012

Plumwood, Val. 1993. *Feminism and the Mastery of Nature* (London: Routledge)

Preston, Christopher. 2012. 'Beyond the end of nature: SRM and two tales of artificiality for the Anthropocene', *Ethics, Policy & Environment*, 15(2): 188–201, https://doi.org/10.1080/21550085.2012.685571

——. 2013. 'Ethics and geoengineering: Reviewing the moral issues raised by solar radiation management and carbon dioxide removal', *Wiley Interdisciplinary Reviews: Climate Change*, 4(1): 23–37, https://doi.org/10.1002/wcc.198

Rayner, Steve. 2010. 'Trust and the transformation of energy systems', *Energy Policy*, 38(6): 2617–23, https://doi.org/10.1016/j.enpol.2009.05.035

Robock, Alan, Kirsten Jerch, and Martin Bunzl. 2008. '20 reasons why geoengineering may be a bad idea', *Bulletin of the Atomic Scientists*, 64(2): 14–59, https://doi.org/10.1080/00963402.2008.11461140

Rolston III, Holmes. 1988. *Environmental Ethics: Duties to and Values in the Natural World* (Philadelphia: Temple University Press)

Rudner, Richard. 1953. 'The scientist qua scientist makes value judgements', *The Philosophy of Science*, 20(1): 1–6

Sandler, Ronald, and John Basl (eds). 2013. *Designer Biology: The Ethics of Intensively Engineering Biological and Ecological Systems* (Lanham: Lexington Press)

Scharping, Nathaniel. 2022. 'Large-scale reforestation efforts could dry out landscapes across the world', *Eos*, http://eos.org/articles/large-scale-reforestation-efforts-could-dry-out-landscapes-across-the-world

Schneider, Linda, and Lili Fuhr. 2020. 'Defending a failed status quo: The case against geoengineering from a civil society perspective', in *Has It Come To This?*, ed. by J. P. Sapinski, Holly Jean Buck, and Andreas Malm (New Brunswick: Rutgers University Press), 50–68. https://doi.org/10.36019/9781978809390-004

Schuppert, Fabian, and Christian Seidel. 2017. 'Feasibility, normative heuristics and the proper place of historical responsibility—A reply to Ohndorf et Al.', *Climatic Change*, 140(2): 101–7, https://doi.org/10.1007/s10584-016-1861-4

Shepherd, John, Ken Caldeira, Peter Cox, Joanna Haigh, David Keith, Brian Launder, Georgina Mace, et al. 2009. *Geoengineering the Climate: Science, Governance, and Uncertainty*, http://royalsociety.org/policy/publications/2009/geoengineering-climate

Shue, Henry. 1993. 'Subsistence emissions and luxury emissions', *Law & Policy*, 15(1): 39–60, https://doi.org/10.1111/j.1467-9930.1993.tb00093.x

——. 2017. 'Climate dreaming: Negative emissions, risk transfer, and irreversibility', *Journal of Human Rights and the Environment*, 8(2): 203–16, https://doi.org/10.4337/jhre.2017.02.02

——. 2018. 'Mitigation gambles: Uncertainty, urgency and the last gamble possible', *Philosophical Transactions of the Royal Society A: Mathematical, Physical and Engineering Sciences*, 376(2119): 20170105, https://doi.org/10.1098/rsta.2017.0105

——. 2019. 'Subsistence protection and mitigation ambition: Necessities, economic and climatic', *The British Journal of Politics and International Relations*, 21(2): 251–62, https://doi.org/10.1177/1369148118819071

——. 2021. *The Pivotal Generation: Why We Have a Moral Responsibility to Slow Climate Change Right Now* (Princeton: Princeton University Press)

Steffen, Will, Johan Rockström, Katherine Richardson, Timothy M. Lenton, Carl Folke, Diana Liverman, Colin P. Summerhayes, Anthony D. Barnosky, Sarah E. Cornell, Michel Crucifix, Jonathan F. Donges, Ingo Fetzer, Steven J. Lade, Marten Scheffer, Ricarda Winkelmann, and Hans Joachim Schellnhuber. 2018. 'Trajectories of the Earth system in the Anthropocene', *Proceedings of the National Academy of Sciences*, 115(33): 8252–59, https://doi.org/10.1073/pnas.1810141115

Sunstein, Cass R. 2010. 'Irreversibility*', *Law, Probability and Risk*, 9(3–4): 227–45, https://doi.org/10.1093/lpr/mgq010

Swierstra, Tsjalling, Dirk Stemerding, and Marianne Boenink. 2009. 'Exploring techno-moral change: The case of the obesity pill', in *Evaluating New Technologies*, ed. by Paul Sollie and Marcus Düwell (Dordrecht: Springer), 119–38, https://doi.org/10.1007/978-90-481-2229-5_9

Szerszynski, Bronislaw, Matthew Kearnes, Phil Macnaghten, Richard Owen, and Jack Stilgoe. 2013. 'Why solar radiation management geoengineering and democracy won't mix', *Environment and Planning A: Economy and Space*, 45(12): 2809–16, https://doi.org/10.1068/a45649

Taebi, Behnam. 2021. *Ethics and Engineering. An Introduction* (Cambridge: Cambridge University Press)

Taebi, Behnam, Jan H. Kwakkel, and Céline Kermisch. 2020. 'Governing climate risks in the face of normative uncertainties', *WIREs Climate Change*, 11(5): e666, https://doi.org/10.1002/wcc.666

Urry, John. 2015. 'Climate change and society', in *Why the Social Sciences Matter*, ed. by Jonathan Michie and Cary L. Cooper (London: Palgrave Macmillan UK), 45–59, https://doi.org/10.1057/9781137269928_4

Vogel, Steven. 2015. *Thinking Like a Mall. Environmental Philosophy after the End of Nature* (Cambridge, MA: MIT Press)

Wagner, Gernot. 2021. *Geoengineering: The Gamble* (Cambridge: Polity Press)

Whyte, Kyle Powys. 2012. 'Now this! Indigenous sovereignty, political obliviousness and governance models for SRM research', *Ethics, Policy & Environment*, 15(2): 172–87, https://doi.org/10.1080/21550085.2012.685570

——. 2017. 'Is it colonial déjà vu? Indigenous peoples and climate injustice', in *Humanities for the Environment: Integrating Knowledge, Forging New Constellations of Practice*, ed. by Joni Adamson and Michael Davis (London; New York: Routledge), 88–105

Wiredu, Kwasi. 1994. 'Philosophy, humankind and the environment', in *Philosophy, Humanity, and Ecology*, ed. by H. Odera Oruka (Nairobi: ACTS Press)

5. Ectogestative Technology and the Beginning of Life

Lead authors: *Lily Eva Frank, Julia Hermann*[1]
Contributing authors: *Llona Kavege, Anna Puzio*

How could ectogestative technology disrupt gender roles, parenting practices, and concepts such as 'birth', 'body', or 'parent'? In this chapter, we situate this emerging technology in the context of the history of reproductive technologies and analyse the potential social and conceptual disruptions to which it could contribute. An ectogestative device, better known as 'artificial womb', enables the extra-uterine gestation of a human being, or mammal more generally. It is currently developed with the main goal of improving the survival chances of extremely premature neonates. We argue that the intended use of the technology in neonatal intensive care units, as an alternative to current incubators ('partial-ectogestation'), challenges concepts such as 'birth', 'fetus', and 'neonate', and has several ethico-legal implications. We moreover address a more futuristic scenario where the entire embryological and fetal development could happen within an artificial womb ('full-ectogestation'). Such a scenario reveals the disruption of gender roles, parenting practices, and concepts such as 'mother', 'father', and 'parent'.

---

[1] All authors contributed original text to this chapter, commented on parts written by others and approved the final version. LEF and JH are the lead authors of this chapter. They coordinated the writing process and did the final editing. LEF wrote the first version of Section 5.2 and contributed to Section 5.3.2. JH wrote the first version of Section 5.3.2 and contributed to all other sections. LK wrote the first version of the introduction. LK and AP together wrote the first version of Section 5.3.1 and Section 5.4.

Both full- and partial-ectogestation would have implications for engineering and design, law-making, ethics, and philosophical anthropology.

Fig. 5.1 Artificial womb. Credit: Menah Wellen

5.1 Introduction

The topic of reproduction touches on an inherent and central aspect of human existence. Humans across time and space have associated fertility with divine powers and have shrouded the beginning of life with mystical origins. In parallel, some of the key developments that have shaped reproductive medicine have increasingly sought to tame, probe, tinker, uncover, and control the mysteries of reproduction and the womb (Romanis et al., 2020).

Throughout the twentieth century, scientists and physicians portrayed the first incubators for early premature neonates as a means 'to replace rather than enhance' maternal[2] connection (Horn, 2020). Similarly, ultrasound checks during pregnancy were introduced in 1956, and while they enable predictions of the sex of the fetus and screenings for any congenital abnormalities, ultrasound has also been weaponized as a personhood-deciding machine in the abortion debate. Ultrasound images enable the outside world to get a view into the womb, yet should not be seen as a mere window into the womb, as they present the first image of the fetus, as a single entity, distinct from its mother (Verbeek, 2008; Mills, 2014). According to Verbeek (2008), the fetus is thereby constituted both as a person and as a patient. In the 1960s, the contraceptive pill disrupted social norms by divorcing sex from reproduction for many women. The role of the maternal womb was once again challenged in 1978 when the first IVF baby Louise Brown saw the light, demonstrating that scientific prowess could overcome and control the wonders of conception beyond the womb. Current techniques enable researchers to culture embryos in vitro for longer than 14 days. Despite the so-called '14-day rule', which is an international ethical standard that was first introduced in the UK by the Warnock Report (1984) and which forbids research on embryos past this point, the limit is increasingly being called into question (McCully, 2021). Consequently, with the track record of biomedicine, the advent of artificial wombs and the complete dissociation of reproduction from the maternal body might seem the next logical step of science's triumph over human biology (Rifkin, 2002).

In this chapter, we situate ectogestative technology in the context of the history of reproductive technologies, and analyze some of the potential social and conceptual disruptions to which this emerging technology could contribute. But what is an ectogestative device (artificial womb)? Simply put, it is a device that enables the extra-uterine gestation of a human being, or mammal more generally.[3] The first recorded mention

---

2   Throughout this chapter we use maternal/mother/motherhood/pregnant woman but recognize that transgender men and nonbinary people can also become pregnant and give birth. Using the 'traditional' terminology in this chapter highlights some of the more striking disruptions that this technology could usher in, including gender roles, family structure, and understanding of gender identity.

3   Our focus in this chapter is on the development of ectogestative technologies for human beings, but a note on its potential use for animals is in place. There are, for

of an artificial womb stems from the sixteenth-century writings of Swiss physician Paracelsus (Grafton, 1999). Four centuries later, British biologist J. B. S. Haldane revisited the topic of artificial wombs in a 1923 lecture. He coined the term 'ectogenesis' to describe the complete process of extra-uterine gestation of a human being from fertilization to birth. Stemming from the Greek words *'ecto-'* and *'genesis'* it literally reads as 'outside development'. Haldane predicted ectogenesis would list amongst the most important discoveries of human history and propel radical social change such as emancipating women from the biological necessity of pregnancy for reproduction (Schwartz, 2019; Haldane, 1924). However, as with several major technological developments, artificial wombs gained traction through fiction like Aldous Huxley's 1932 dystopian novel *Brave New World* and more recent feminist accounts, such as Helen Sedgwick's *The Growing Season* (2017) and Rebecca Ann Smith's *Baby X* (2016).

While film and literature may have the public dreaming about far future technologies, recent biomedical developments suggest that machine-mediated gestation no longer resides solely in the sphere of science fiction. Today, development at conception (with IVF techniques) and towards the late end of the gestation period (from ~24 weeks out of a typical pregnancy of 40 weeks, due to high-tech neonatal incubators) can already occur outside of the maternal body (Singer and Wells, 2006). As such, while full ectogenesis is still out of reach, partial-ectogestation, 'the partial development of new mammals outside the maternal body, where normally this development happens inside', is already a reality (Kingma and Finn, 2019: 356).

Notwithstanding the location, the *kind* of development that occurs ex utero is also an important aspect of research and controversy. The advances in neonatal intensive care now enable premature neonates to survive; however, for extremely premature neonates born under 28 weeks, chances of survival drop and the transition to independent life is often complicated by the immaturity of organs such as the lungs,

---

instance, efforts being made to develop an artificial womb that can be of use in the endeavor to bring back the extinct mammoth ('de-extinction') (see e.g. Rohwer and Marris, 2018). It should also be noted that one of the ethical issues raised by the development of ectogestative technology for human beings is the use of animals in the research process. We thank Bernice Bovenkerk for drawing our attention to these points.

guts, heart, and the brain (Lincetto & Banerjee, 2020). This often leads to lifelong physical and mental health complications (van der Hout-van der Jagt et al., 2022). The lack of improvement in extremely premature survival has indicated to many researchers that neonatal intensive care has reached a threshold of efficacy with ventilation-based life-support, and thus researchers have endeavored to develop alternative therapeutic means to improve survival. To this end, in 1997 at Juntendo University (Japan) Dr. Yoshinori Kuwabara and his team developed an extra-uterine fetal incubation system (EUFI) and were able to transfer fetal goats out of the doe's womb and maintain them in fetal physiology submerged in a box with artificial amniotic fluid. Unfortunately, the goats were not able to survive the transition once removed from the device (Gelfand, 2006).

Twenty years later though, in 2017, a team at Philadelphia Children's Hospital developed the 'biobag', a hermetically-sealed pouch that successfully enabled the transfer and gestation of fetal lambs to term (Partridge et al., 2017). A similar device, EVE or the 'ex vivo uterine environment therapy' was also successfully developed by an Australian-Japanese team (Usada et al., 2019). In both devices, the lambs float in artificial amniotic fluid and the umbilical cord is preserved and connected by a cannulation system to an external device, providing nutrients and oxygenating the blood, thus serving as placenta. In addition, the system is pumpless meaning the fetal heart alone powers the circuit, replicating in utero conditions and blood circulation (Partridge et al., 2017; Usada et al., 2019). In 2019, a multidisciplinary team of researchers at Eindhoven University of Technology (The Netherlands) set out to design and develop the PLS or 'Perinatal Life Support System' aimed at extremely preterm human neonates in the coming decades (CORDIS, 2019; Verweij et al., 2021).

As it stands, these devices are solely meant to serve as a therapeutic alternative to standard neonatal intensive care. Current researchers do not aim to push the limits of viability or carry out full-ectogestation. In the following sections, we argue that the intended use of the technology in neonatal intensive care units challenges concepts such as 'birth', 'fetus', and 'neonate', and has several ethico-legal implications. We moreover address a more futuristic scenario where the entire embryological and fetal development could happen within a technological device ('full-ectogestation'). Any claims related to full-ectogestation are highly speculative. Apart from the fact that we do not know whether it will ever be technically possible, we also do not know how safe it would be for the fetus, how it would affect parent-child bonding, how expensive it would be, who could afford it, and so forth. Given the fast pace of technological development and the human tendency to push things further, philosophers, designers and artists are creating and reflecting upon possible scenarios. The use of technomoral scenarios (see Boenink, Swierstra and Stemerding, 2010) to anticipate possible disruptions related to full-ectogestation can help to get a clearer idea of what is at stake when developing this technology and what would be (un)desirable. The scenario we address below (Section 5.3.2) reveals the potential disruption of gender roles, parenting practices, and concepts such as 'mother', 'father', and 'parent'.

In our own research, we have, together with a speculative designer, organized stakeholder workshops, in which the discussion of technomoral scenarios was combined with prototyping activities. One of the issues addressed in relation to a technomoral scenario around partial-ectogestation was how parents could connect to the human being in the ectogestative device and whether the device should be portable, transparent, located in a hospital or at home.[4] Both full- and partial-ectogestation have implications for engineering and design, law-making, ethics, and philosophical anthropology, to which we will return in the final section (Section 5.4).

5.2 Impacts and social disruptions

The development of ectogestative technology could usher in several impacts and social disruptions, divided here into three broad categories: 1) gender roles and the family, 2) moralization and de-moralization, and 3) medicalization. This section is divided into two parts, the first focusing on partial-ectogestation and the second on full-ectogestation. Although

---

4   We collaborated with speculative designer Lisa Mandemaker in a project funded by ESDiT and DesignLab Twente. The following people participated in this collaborative research and design project: Patricia de Vries, Lily Eva Frank, Margoth González Woge, Naomi Jacobs, Julia Hermann, Llona Kavege, Lisa Mandemaker, Sabine Wildevuur, and Cristina Zaga.

already partial-ectogestation challenges gender roles and the family to some extent, this is mainly the case for full-ectogestation, which is why we discuss this category only under full-ectogestation (Section 5.2.2).

5.2.1 Partial-ectogestation

Moralization and de-moralization

Ectogestative technology could contribute to the moralization of certain issues, and to the de-moralization of others. Moralization is the phenomenon by which something that was at one point considered to be a morally neutral choice, act or state of character changes into something that is evaluated from a moral perspective, within a particular society. De-moralization is the opposite process: what used to be considered morally right or wrong comes to be regarded as morally neutral. A classic example of moralization is the shift from smoking being seen merely as a matter of personal preference to a habit that is the object of social disgust and moral judgment, especially when one's smoking impacts the health of others (second hand smoke) (see e.g. Eriksen, 2020). An example of de-moralization is the process in which, in some parts of the world, sexual preferences came to be seen as neither right or wrong.

The process of moralization is not in and of itself morally good or bad; this requires an independent evaluation. However, many of the decisions that pregnant people make are heavily moralized. The negative effects of alcohol on the developing fetus mounted and public awareness spread, starting in the 1970s. Since then, drinking alcohol during pregnancy has become increasingly moralized in many Western societies, particularly in the United States. Pregnant women who drink (or use drugs) are judged not only as doing something unhealthy, but as doing something morally wrong. Similar patterns surround consumption of certain foods, being overweight, opting for elective cesarean section instead of vaginal delivery, and, after birth, choosing formula or breastfeeding.

Considering the many ways in which the choices of pregnant women and new mothers/parents are moralized, it seems likely that the introduction of ectogestative technology could come with further moralization. As stated earlier, partial-ectogestation is intended to be used to mitigate the health impacts of being born prematurely. When a new medical intervention or technology comes into use, its very existence as an option changes the range of decisions with moral import that a patient can make. New options for care can be experienced as burdensome, forcing people to make medical decisions that would not have previously been available to them. For example, prenatal genetic testing gives pregnant people more information about the traits their fetus carries allowing them to choose to terminate their pregnancy (Verbeek, 2009). Other people may experience this new information and the new choices that it presents them with as liberating. The possibility of using ectogestative technology for fetuses that would otherwise be born prematurely and face risks of death and disability will mediate the choices that the prospective parents can make. These choices are likely to be seen as heavily morally laden. The phenomenon of the 'technological imperative' in health care may intensify these effects, although the influence of this effect will likely vary widely between different types of health care settings and national and cultural contexts (Koenig, 1988). The technological imperative has been observed by social scientists of medicine, who argue that once an advanced technology is introduced into medical care, physicians and hospitals feel a mandate to use them, regardless of whether or not they serve the patient's interests (Koenig, 1988; Rothman, 1997; Hofmann, 2002).

Medicalization

Ectogestative technology can be expected to accelerate the process of medicalization of pregnancy and giving birth. Medicalization is the phenomenon by which a condition, behaviour, or physical/mental state changes from being a matter of choice or mere difference to being a matter which can be described, labeled, and potentially treated by doctors. Medicalization is not inherently positive or negative. Two classic examples illustrate this. The medicalization of certain mental health conditions like schizophrenia has shifted the way people understand those suffering from the condition away from seeing them as evil, possessed by spirits, or defective in character, to seeing them as people with a medical condition. This also comes with the possibility of researching and discovering treatments, medications, and therapies which may help to relieve the suffering and include patients in the community. Arguably, this form of medicalization, which moved certain mental maladies from being seen as personal or spiritual defects to psychological problems has on balance been a good thing for the well-being of these individuals (Conrad and Schneider, 1992). On the other hand, medicalization has been used to obfuscate injustices or recast human responses to their conditions as medical problems, e.g. drapetomania, the 'mental illness' that caused enslaved African people to tend to run away (Myers, 2014). In many places in the world, homosexuality is still labelled a disease.

Pregnancy and birth have been heavily medicalized in many WEIRD (Western, educated, industrialized, rich and democratic) countries and this medicalization has been subject to critiques, particularly by feminist thinkers (e.g. Rothman, 1991; Harley, 1993; Cahill, 2001; Beech and Phipps, 2008; Nisha, 2021), who are suspicious of the transfer of power and decision making surrounding pregnancy from pregnant women and their midwives to a patriarchal, technological, male-dominated medical establishment.[5] The development of partial-ectogestation is likely to contribute to further medicalization of pregnancy and birth. Assuming that the chances for survival and a life without severe handicaps would increase significantly, it can be expected that pregnancies would be monitored even more closely than they are now and the numbers of extremely premature babies in neonatal intensive care units would rise. This of course also depends on the costs of the technology.

5.2.2 Full-ectogestation

Gender roles and the family

Ectogestative technology, particularly full-ectogestation, could cause disruptions to dominant gender roles in families and in parenting practices, which remain strong around the world despite women's participation in the labor market. From a feminist perspective, such

---

5   Of course this is a major simplification, given that, for example, there are significant differences between countries in the European Union and the UK. C.f. Perrot and Horn (2022).

disruptions would be desirable. In many families, women still do the majority of child care and are assumed to have a special kind of bond with infants and children. As care ethicist Joan Tronto (1993: 103) points out, care is often 'described and defined as a necessary relationship between two individuals, most often a mother and a child [...] leading to a romanticization of mother and child, so that they become like a romantic couple in contemporary Western discourse'. If this special bond is partially constituted or justified by the fact that biological mothers 'carried the baby' inside their body for nine months of gestation, then full-ectogestation may challenge this assumption. A concern cited in the literature is that of a perceived threat to mother-child or maternal-fetal bonding that could be posed if the fetus spends some or all of its development in the ectogestative device instead of inside, or as part of, the maternal body (Landau 2007; de Bie et al., 2022; Lubetzky, 2020). Changes to the process of maternal-fetal bonding may challenge gender roles and the family because the nine months of pregnancy have historically been one of the purportedly scientific justifications for the special relationship between mother and infant (Creanley, 1981; Leifer, 1980). Thus, to the extent that this process is disrupted or perceived to be disrupted by ectogestative technology, gender roles in parenting may shift.

Maternal-fetal bonding (sometimes called attachment) can be defined as 'an abstract concept, representing the affiliative relationship between a parent and a fetus, which is potentially present before pregnancy, is related to cognitive and emotional abilities to conceptualize another human being, and develops within an ecological system' (Doan and Zimerman, 2008: 110). Concerns about the disruption of this process have to do with the long-term psycho-social development of the child, the trusting relationship between the parent and the child, and even impacts on fetal physiology (brain structure). The mechanisms of prenatal bonding and their impact on postnatal bonding are complex and mediated by a wide variety of factors, such as maternal stress and anxiety, as well as social support (Göbel et al., 2018). For example, Alhusen's (2008) literature review on the topic identified multiple variables that have been hypothesized to impact maternal-fetal bonding and been empirically researched, such as demographic factors (e.g. maternal age), 'perception of fetal movement', presence of mood disorders in the mother, substance use during pregnancy, and previous pregnancy loss (Alhusen, 2008: 319).

There is mixed evidence that the use of technology can impact maternal-fetal bonding. For example, research by Ji et al. (2005) shows that pregnant women who were shown three-dimensional versus two-dimensional ultrasound images of their fetus showed greater signs of increased maternal-fetal bonding, such as being able to form a 'mental picture' of their baby, and were more likely to feel that they already 'knew' the baby when it was born.

Full-ectogestation could potentially open opportunities for fathers to have stronger bonds with their babies, freed from the expectation that they have a more distanced relationship with their child compared to the parent that gave birth. In homosexual or queer relationships, this may further equalize the parenting roles. It has to be noted though that there are no universal family structures or gender roles. There are significant cross-cultural differences in the structure of the family. The nuclear family, in which a male and female parent live together and raise children, is not a universal phenomenon. Nor is the structure in which the mother plays the role of main caregiver universal (Ruspini, 2015). We are here focusing on the possible disruptions to the Western paradigm, thereby acknowledging that the disruptive effects of this technology are likely to be different in other contexts. For instance, in more communal societies, the role of raising children is distributed among many people, including not only relatives but also neighbors and other inhabitants of the same community. However, it is usually women who play this role (see e.g. Edwards, 2000).[6]

Moralization and de-moralization

Further research would be needed to understand how the development of full-ectogestation may create instances of new moralization. People wishing to have a biological child may face social and moral pressure

---

6   Current research on ectogestative technology takes place primarily in the United States (Partridge et al., 2017), Europe (Verweij, 2022), Australia (Miura et al., 2015), and Japan (IToH, 2010). There is to our knowledge no philosophical or ethical literature available from the Japanese context, which is why we focus on potential disruptions to the Western paradigm.

to use ectogestative technology. Although at this point, this is merely speculation, moral pressure could arise because it could *seem* to provide a safer and more controlled environment for fetal development than the maternal body. The fetus can be exposed to fewer risks and can be continuously monitored. On the other hand, the possibility of full-ectogestation could create the opposite kind of social and moral pressure. Choosing 'natural' pregnancy might be characterized as the more virtuous choice.[7] Women who use ectogestative technology conversely might be painted as selfish, cold, or lazy. Within the workplace, opting for a 'natural' pregnancy over ectogestation may be viewed negatively from the perspective of productivity and ambition. Taking the needed parental leave to deliver and recover from pregnancy may be seen as selfish, afterall in many professions this time off puts additional burdens on co-workers to pick up the slack. Employers could thus demand that their employees work more. Hooton and Romanis (2022) have recently argued that the field of employment law will need to address ectogestation and that the reproductive rights of employees with respect to employers should not be 'stratified' or understood any differently depending on the bio-technological interventions that they use to reproduce.

One new area in which moralization may play a role and which has been extensively discussed in the emerging literature on the ethics of ectogestation is abortion. Induced abortion is defined in the medical literature as a procedure, either medical or surgical, which ends a pregnancy (Blackshaw and Rodger, 2019; Cohen, 2017; Räsänen, 2017). As Cohen explains, the possibility of ectogenesis (prima facie) removes the most morally and legally influential justification for a woman's right to an abortion — bodily autonomy based on the presumption of gestational parenthood. If the termination of a pregnancy no longer necessarily involves the death of the embryo or fetus, the societal (and potentially conceptual) disruptions could involve changes in the meaning of abortion itself, changes in the moral and legal permissibility

---

7   We use quotation marks here to signal that the term 'natural' is problematic. Given the role that technology has come to play in this context (think of ultrasound, prenatal diagnostics, IVF, pre implementation diagnostics, c-sections, etc.), we can ask ourselves how 'natural' a normal pregnancy actually is.

of abortion, and changes in the moral rights and responsibilities of genetic parents.

We can also envisage processes of de-moralization, e.g., regarding the behaviour of becoming mothers. If full-ectogestation were to become a reality and the mother's behaviour ceased to have a direct effect on the development of the fetus, it would probably not be judged in moral terms anymore.

Medicalization

Full-ectogestation would allow for more and earlier medical interventions on the developing fetus. It may also allow for the environment to be optimized for a variety of growth and developmental factors, and for the fetal development and the environment to be constantly monitored to look for early signs of abnormalities, distress, or ways in which the environment could be improved. Ectogestation might also create opportunities for simple forms of human enhancement, for example, by allowing longer gestation times, which are associated with better cognitive capacities (Vollmer and Edmonds, 2019).

5.3 Conceptual disruption

Intricately related to the potential social impacts and disruptions just described, we can imagine several conceptual disruptions. Again we will start with disruptions related to partial-ectogestation and subsequently address disruptions that full-ectogestation might lead to. While already the advent of partial-ectogestation challenges concepts related to the beginning of life, body and personhood, full-ectogestation can be expected to disrupt concepts related to the family, gender, and parenthood. It should be noted that earlier reproductive technologies, as well as developments in medical science, also contributed to conceptual disruptions. Ectogestative technology is thus not unique in this respect, but it seems to exacerbate these processes of disruption.

5.3.1 Partial-ectogestation

Beginning of life

The advent of partial-ectogestation will challenge existing concepts and biological classifications around the beginning of life. Birth has historically stood for the detachment of the offspring from its mother's womb and the beginning of independent life. However, partial-ectogestation will turn a coetaneous physical and physiological process into a fragmented one, consisting of two distinct events. The first event — 'birth-by-location change' — would happen when the fetus is separated from the maternal body and translocated to an ectogestative device. Because the device maintains fetal physiology ex utero, the second event, namely 'birth-by-physiology change' would only occur after extrication from the machine and successful transition to neonatal stage by breathing in oxygen from the air into the lungs and feeding through the mouth instead of the umbilical cord (Kingma and Finn, 2020).

The significance of birth is not limited to medical classification or social purposes, such as birthdays. Birth is also the moment at which *some* changes in the legal and moral standing of the infant occur. Before birth, in many legal systems, viability is the point at which the fetus gains the status of an individual with rights distinct from the pregnant person. In medical contexts, this means that physicians have responsibilities to the fetus as a patient distinct from the mother and may even conceive of the possibility of so-called 'maternal-fetal conflicts' occurring (Fasouliotis and Schenker, 2000). But birth itself also carries legal significance, for example, one standard means of determining whether neonaticide has occurred forensically is examining the lungs for evidence that the infant was 'born alive' or took its first breath (Phillips and Ong, 2018). In many places, parental responsibility and decision-making rights also shift legally after birth. While 'inside' the maternal body, medical care decisions about the fetus may be the responsibility of both parents, but are the right of the pregnant woman to make. After birth, if a second parent is present (usually genetic parent, in the male, cis-hetero case), he has an equal legal right to make medical decisions about the care of the newborn.

The socio-moral significance of birth can also be inferred from the complex ways in which people in many societies experience and react to the loss of life of the fetus (miscarriage) versus early infant death. Ectogestation complicates matters as experts will have to come together and decide which birth (birth-by-location change or birth-by-physiology change) should take normative precedence. This decision will have strong ethico-legal implications for the abortion debate, medical decision-making in obstetric care, and maternal-fetal conflicts.

Moreover, if a premature fetus is partially born and transferred to an ectogestative device, meaning born-by-location change but not yet born-by-physiology change, then the appropriate term to refer to the human offspring inside the device necessitates re-evaluation. Developing humans are categorized as fetuses from the eighth week of gestation (Cleveland Clinic, 2020). When a fetus leaves the womb, it becomes a neonate or newborn. An offspring born preterm in the neonatal intensive care unit is still considered a neonate, for it must shoulder the burden of its own life, albeit with some assistance. However, the offspring in the ectogestative device follows a different creative and formative process, and while ex utero, it functions 'as if the neonate had never been born' (Romanis, 2018: 753). Recent literature on the metaphysics of pregnancy has also argued, based on metabolic, immunological, and topological grounds, that fetuses are more than just babies gestating in their maternal host. They are a developing *part* of their pregnant mothers and only become separate individual entities post-birth (Kingma, 2019). Consequently, ectogestation and the specific developmental stage before birth-by-physiology change may require a new term to distinguish the ex utero gestating offspring from fetus and neonate. We will return to this point in Section 5.4.

Body and personhood

Ectogestative technology gives rise to a re-examination of anthropological concepts, a re-negotiation of what it means to be a human being or a person. The technology challenges our previous ideas of human being, body, and personhood. The boundaries between animate and inanimate, between nature and culture/technology, human and non-human, body and technology become blurred. How can we redraw these boundaries responsibly? Ectogestative technology is changing the understanding of the body. For example, it raises the question whether the ectogestative device is really completely separate from the human body or could be seen as an extension of it (Puzio, 2022: 291–346). Disability studies, for example, have argued that technology is perceived as part of the body by those who are existentially dependent on it (wheelchairs, pacemakers, implants, etc.) (Graham, 1999: 119; Thweatt, 2016: 152; 2018: 371). Whether ectogestative technology is considered as being part of the body can be relevant for legal issues, such as the protection of the mother and her decision about her own body. Moreover, like other technologies, such as prostheses, ectogestative technology can be seen as something different from a mere imitation or extension of the human body. It challenges our understanding of the concept of the 'human body' as something individual, natural, or purely biological and in contrast with that which is social, cultural, or technological.

Similar to obstetric ultrasound, ectogestative technology affects the concept of personhood. According to Verbeek's analysis of ultrasound technology, it contributes to the constitution of the fetus both as a patient and as a person (Verbeek, 2008). Arguably, by not only making the fetus appear as a being that is distinct from its mother, but actually forming an environment in which it can exist and develop independently of its mother, ectogestative technology contributes to the constitution of the fetus as a person (and patient) in an even stronger sense. This challenges the concept of personhood: who and what should count as a person?

5.3.2 Full-ectogestation

Parenthood

A cluster of concepts that is likely to be affected by full-ectogestation in particular is mother-father-parent-family-gender. Here we focus on the concept 'mother', while emphasizing that other concepts in the cluster are also affected. The concept of mother can be analyzed as having at least three different dimensions: genetic, gestational, and social mother (see Ber, 2000). Usually, people conceive of mothers as being mothers along all three dimensions. The three dimensions can come apart, however (see Fig. 5.2). A woman who has adopted a child is the child's social mother, but not its genetic or gestational mother. A woman who has made use of surrogacy is the child's genetic and social mother, but not its gestational mother. She could also be just the social mother, in case she made use of egg donation (see Fig. 5.2 for the different possible combinations). It should also be noted that social motherhood can be shared. The differentiations depicted in the table below are to a large extent due to the development of reproductive technologies, such as egg donation and IVF. The table contains three types of women who are mothers, though not gestational mothers: adoptive mothers or foster mothers, women who used surrogacy, and egg donors. This shows that also in the absence of the availability of full-ectogestation, becoming a mother without gestating a child is possible. Nevertheless, this technology poses a challenge to the concept of mother, by potentially creating the possibility for having a child without there being any gestational mother at all.

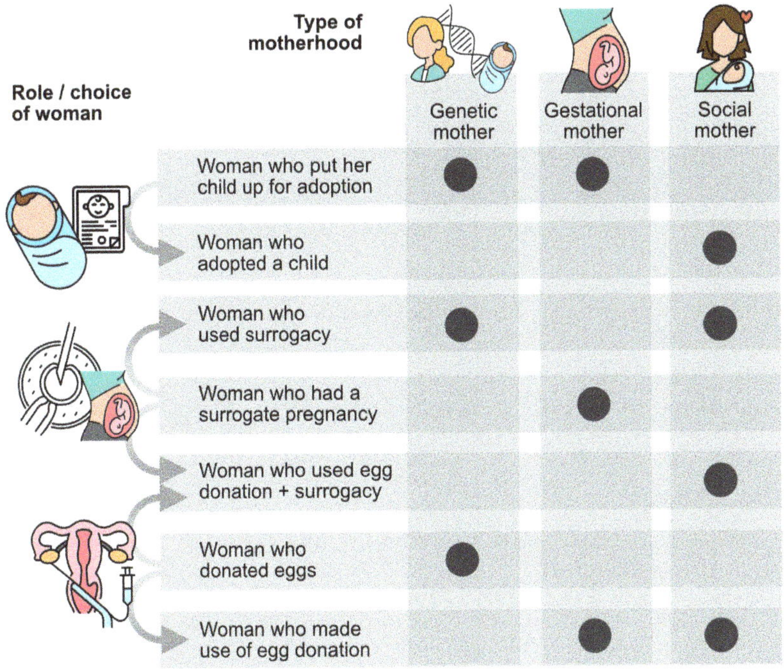

Role / choice of woman	Type of motherhood	Genetic mother	Gestational mother	Social mother
	Woman who put her child up for adoption	●	●	
	Woman who adopted a child			●
	Woman who used surrogacy	●		●
	Woman who had a surrogate pregnancy		●	
	Woman who used egg donation + surrogacy			●
	Woman who donated eggs	●		
	Woman who made use of egg donation		●	●

Fig. 5.2 Different types of motherhood. Credit: Ilse Oosterlaken

If the possibility of full-ectogestation were to become reality, there could be children who had only genetic and social mothers but no gestational mothers (see Jacobs, 2023). We can imagine a group of people raising a child together, where some of them might be the child's genetic parents, while none of them is a gestational mother. In such a scenario, the question arises as to what makes a parent a mother as opposed to a father. If we think of a non-binary person being one of the parents of the child, is that person a mother or a father? While on our current understanding of motherhood, only female persons can be mothers, this scenario raises the question as to why being female should be a necessary condition for being a mother. The scenario invites speculation about whether we would still need the concept 'mother' at all or could replace both 'mother' or 'father' by 'parent'.[8]

As mentioned above, full-ectogestation would also affect related concepts, such as 'gender' and 'family'. The possible social disruptions discussed in the previous section (disruptions of family structures and gender roles) arguably also involve conceptual disruptions. For instance, by changing parenting practices and family constellations, the technology might have the potential to disrupt the Western concept of the nuclear family. In addition, the disruption of traditional gender roles affects the concept of gender, which is partly constituted by these roles.

5.4 Looking ahead

The further development of ectogestative technology has implications for engineering and design, law-making,[9] ethics, and philosophical

---

8   For a problematization of definitions of 'mother' and the categorization of people as mothers (instead of parents) see Haslanger (2014: 30f).

9   *Legal and social conventions around birth*: ectogestative technology can be expected to affect the conventions that we find in different cultures. For instance, legal and social conventions surrounding the date of birth differ culturally and have varied over time. For example, in Chinese culture, a baby's first birthday occurs on the day they are born: they are already one year old. Whereas in western culture a baby's first birthday occurs a year after they are born (Sullivan and Liu-Sullivan, 2021). In 2023 South Korea's government officially changed the way citizen's ages are calculated, shifting from infants being designated one year old at birth and two years old on January 1 of the first year of life, to a system which marks ages with the passing of birth days (Tong-Hyung, 2023). In Bhutan, traditionally, birthdays are not routinely

anthropology. Anticipating how the advent of ectogestation may disrupt various aspects of society and our notion of the beginning of life can be of use to designers, engineers, and ethicists alike in the research and implementation process. As mentioned above, concepts such as 'birth', 'fetus' and 'neonate' will need to be reevaluated. Partial-ectogestation in particular may introduce a novel development stage between fetus and neonate, which requires new terminology. To this end, several terms have begun to circulate in the literature, including 'gestateling' (Romanis, 2018), 'fetonate' (De Bie et al., 2022), and 'perinate' (Van der Hout-van der Jagt et al., 2022).

The disruption of birth occasioned both by practically fragmenting the process and conceptually clouding the distinction between fetus and neonate will have implications for ethics, law-making, and even the design of ectogestative devices. Birth is often used to demarcate the point in human development at which full legal personhood is assigned (Mills, 2014; Romanis, 2019). If birth-by-location change is granted the normative significance of birth as traditionally understood, then the ectogestative device will appear more similar to an incubator, harboring a neonate in a liquid environment. This implies that the moment at which full legal and moral status is attributed could remain as it is, namely after delivery from the maternal womb — thus topology wins. However, if birth-by-physiology change is attributed more significance, then the ectogestative device will be more akin to a device that simulates gestation in the maternal womb. Consequently, the gestating human in the device would be closer to a fetus than to a neonate and might only qualify for partial legal and moral status.

Beyond usability, the design of a technology can also be rooted in values that will guide usage and perpetuate encoded norms (Friedman et al., 2002). Thus, design requirements of an ectogestative device should reflect values and norms that we wish to abide by. These values will be informed by how we ontologically make sense of the technology and how it mediates our notion of the human being inside the device. For example, if it is perceived as being similar to a fetus, design priorities will likely lean towards mimicking womb-like conditions. However, if it is perceived as a neonate (but with fetal physiology as described by

---

celebrated and the date of one's birth is not something one necessarily even knows. For administrative purposes, most people share a birthday of January 1st.

the US EXTEND team in De Bie et al., 2022), then extra consideration could be given to building a see-through device, making it portable, and allowing for as much contact as possible, as expected from current incubators. Moreover, if the human being in the device is conceptualized as something other than a fetus or neonate, and rather as a novel stage in human development, then design requirements will also need to be carefully assessed to be in accord with the law, ethics, and social mores.

When analyzing the social disruption brought about by a technology, it is also imperative to acknowledge how the technology is situated in the socio-material environment, as this will shape how it is appropriated. Reproductive technologies have often been lauded as progressive and liberating for many women, however, there has also been an increasing trend in biomedicine to medicalise reproduction, pregnancy, and the maternal body. For example, ultrasounds are disruptive for they can act as 'moral speculum'. Beyond ascertaining the life of a fetus, they can serve as 'personhood-deciding machines' and become a medium for some women to choose for or against a termination of their pregnancy (Mills, 2014). With partial-ectogestation, while the impetus is on saving the extremely premature, we cannot risk effacing pregnant women both from their role in gestation and from stakeholder considerations in the research and design process. After all, it is through their body that we must first go to access the fetus. In addition, regarding full-ectogestation, it has to be kept in mind that the technology would use a lot of energy and there would be the need to justify why limited resources should be used for a device the function of which can, under normal circumstances, also be fulfilled by a female body. Consequently, for both partial and full-ectogestation it is imperative to think about how and where this technology will be situated, and to anticipate its misuse, so it is not introduced to exacerbate current injustices.

Our reflections with stakeholders on a scenario around partial-ectogestation revealed concerns about how to connect with the human being developing ex utero and a dissensus regarding whether the ectogestative device should mimic the maternal womb as much as possible or rather be designed differently, possibly improving upon the natural womb. Our reflections and workshop on more speculative scenarios around full-ectogestation showed that such scenarios seem to make room for an upgrading of fathers, overcoming traditional understandings of the roles and tasks of mothers, a more equal division of care labour and responsibility, and more possibilities for members of the LGBTQ+ community to become parents. They also supported worries about the potential negative effects on parent-child bonding and the physical and mental development of the human being developing ex utero. Given these worries as well those mentioned above concerning market driven pressures on women's choices, one could conclude that an upgrading of fathers etc. should be promoted by other means than full-ectogestation, which is ultimately not desirable. Imagining possible futures with full-ectogestation would then be seen as helping us envision more vividly and forcefully the possibility and desirability of certain changes or disruptions, which we could then try to achieve by other means.

It is, moreover, important to include intercultural voices in the development of ectogestative technology. Attitudes towards the technology and the way it is dealt with will strongly depend on cultural factors and vary greatly according to cultural background. This makes interculturally sensitive development and handling of ectogestative technologies necessary. When it comes to questions of life and its beginning, religions play an important role. Despite the loss of importance of religions in many Western societies, these beliefs have strongly shaped the value systems of these societies, including the understanding of nature, creation, and human beings. As many cultural and religious traditions and rituals are associated with birth, it is likely that with ectogestative technology such rituals will undergo transformation and new rituals will emerge.

Since, as mentioned above, technologies can change our understanding of the human being and the body, they spur novel anthropological reflection. Technologies transport human understandings/conceptions of the human being. Therefore, it is important to critically examine which human understandings and discriminations are transported in technologies. Which patriarchal, sexist, racist, and heteronormative structures are taken over unnoticed in the design of ectogestative devices?

Anthropology is increasingly turning away from essentialist notions of a supposed 'human nature' towards a non-essentialist, dynamic, and fluid understanding of human identity. Assuming that the understanding of the human being is always in a state of flux and is not a constant or essence that transcends time, space, and culture makes it possible to think of it as open to (also technological) change. In particular, movements of thought such as New Materialism and Critical Posthumanism, which have been strongly influenced by Donna Haraway's thinking, are striving to break down old anthropological concepts and dichotomies (of inanimate-animate, human-animal, human-machine, nature-culture/technology, woman-man). Haraway coined the ontological, epistemological, and political figure of the cyborg, which as 'a cybernetic organism, a hybrid of machine and organism' (Haraway, 2004: 7) has a hybrid, fluid, and dynamic identity. The cyborg is neither unequivocally human, nor animal nor machine, thus refusing any categorization and classification, and therefore has a 'subversive potential ... to resist any re-ontologization of the human' (Ruf, 2001: 286; see also Chapter 3). There is no pre-existing 'human nature', but rather being human is produced in relationship and interaction with non-human entities (e.g., technologies or animals). Contemporary anthropology re-locates the position of the human being, valorizes non-human entities, and criticizes anthropocentrism. Critical Posthumanism and New Materialism reflect anew on concepts such as the human, the body, life, nature, matter, etc. They draw attention to the fact that technologies such as ectogestative technology blur the boundaries between animate-inanimate, human-animal, human-machine, nature-culture/technology, woman-man, question these boundaries and want to redraw them responsibly. In doing so, they draw attention to discrimination in these boundary drawing processes and encourage intercultural, anti-racist, and inclusive approaches. They also ask who determines which boundaries are drawn and advocate for the diversity of bodies and genders.

Further listening and watching

Readers who would like to learn more about ectogestative technology as a socially disruptive technology might be interested in listening to the following interviews and a related episode of the ESDiT podcast (https://anchor.fm/esdit):

Julia Hermann, Interview about the ethics of socially disruptive technologies for the Australian radio program *Radical Philosophy*, 3CR Community Radio, 22 January 2022: https://www.3cr.org.au/ radicalphilosophy/episode-202201221330/ethics-socially-disruptive-technologies-dr-julia-hermann

Julia Hermann on 'Ectogestative technology', *Focus*, NPO Radio 1, 7 May 2021:

https://www.nporadio1.nl/podcasts/dekennisvannu/1375886-zwanger-of-een-kind-uit-een- kunst-baarmoeder

Julia Hermann on 'The artificial womb': https://www.esdit.nl/2021/ esdit-podcast-julia-hermann-on-the-artificial-womb/

References

Alhusen, Jeanne L. 2008. 'A literature update on maternal-fetal attachment', *Journal of Obstetric, Gynecologic & Neonatal Nursing, 37*(3), 315–28, https:// doi.org/10.1111/j.1552-6909.2008.00241.x

Beech, Beverley A. Lawrence, and Belinda Phipps. 2008. 'Normal birth: women's stories', in *Normal Childbirth: Evidence and Debate*, ed. by Soo Downe (Elsevier, 2008, second edition), 67–81

Ber, Rosalie. 2000. 'Ethical issues in gestational surrogacy', *Theoretical Medicine and Bioethics*, 21, 153–69, https://doi.org/10.1023/A:1009956218800

Boenink, Marianne, Swierstra, Tsjalling, and Stemerding, Dirk. 2010. 'Anticipating the interaction between technology and morality: A scenario study of experimenting with humans in bionanotechnology', *Studies in Ethics, Law, and Technology*, 4(2). https://doi.org/10.2202/1941-6008.1098

Cahill, Heather A. 2001. 'Male appropriation and medicalization of childbirth: An historical analysis', *Journal of Advanced Nursing, 33*(3), 334–42, https:// doi.org/10.1046/j.1365-2648.2001.01669.x

Cleveland Clinic. 2020. 'Fetal development: Month-by-month stages of pregnancy', *Cleveland Clinic*, https://my.clevelandclinic.org/health/ articles/7247-fetal-development-stages-of-growth

Conrad, Peter, and Joseph W. Schneider. 1992. *Deviance and Medicalization: From Badness to Sickness*. (Temple University Press)

CORDIS European Commission. 2019. 'Brave new world? Artificial womb prototype offering hope for premature babies', *CORDIS EU Research Results*, https://cordis.europa.eu/article/

id/411541-brave-new-world-artificial-womb-prototype-offering-hope-for-premature-babies

Cranley, Mecca S. 1981. 'Development of a tool for the measurement of maternal attachment during pregnancy', *Nursing Research* 30(5), pp. 281–84, https://doi.org/10.1097/00006199-198109000-00008

De Bie, Felix, Sarah Kim, Sourav Bose, Pamela Nathanson, Emily Partridge, Alan Flake, and Chris Feudtner. 2022. 'Ethics considerations regarding artificial womb technology for the fetonate', *The American Journal of Bioethics*, 1–12, https://doi.org/10.1080/15265161.2022.2048738

Doan, Helen, and Anona Zimerman. 2008. 'Prenatal attachment: A developmental model', *International Journal of Prenatal and Perinatal Psychology and Medicine*, 20(1–2), 20–28

Edwards, Arlene E. 2000. 'Community mothering: The relationship between mothering and the community work of Black women', *Journal of the Association for Research on Mothering*, 2(2), 87–100

Fasouliotis, Sozos, and Joseph Schenker. 2000. 'Maternal–fetal conflict', *European Journal of Obstetrics & Gynecology and Reproductive Biology*, 89(1): 101–7, https://doi.org/10.1016/S0301-2115(99)00166-9

Friedman, Batya, Peter H. Kahn, and Alan Borning. 2002. 'Value sensitive design: Theory and methods', *University of Washington Technical Report*, 2–12

Gelfand, Scott. 2006. 'Introduction', in *Ectogenesis: Artificial Womb Technology and the Future of Human Reproduction*, ed. by Scott Gelfand and John Shook (Amsterdam; New York, NY: Brill/Rodopi)

Göbel, Ariane, Lydia Yao Stuhrmann, Susanne Harder, Michael Schulte-Markwort, and Susanne Mudra. 2018. 'The association between maternal-fetal bonding and prenatal anxiety: An explanatory analysis and systematic review', *Journal of Affective Disorders*, 239: 313–27, https://doi.org/10.1016/j.jad.2018.07.024

Grafton, Anthony. 1999. *Natural Particulars: Nature and the Disciplines in Renaissance Europe* (Boston: MIT Press)

Graham, Elaine. 1999. 'Words made flesh: Women, embodiment and practical theology', *Feminist Theology*, 7(21): 109–21, https://doi.org/10.1177/096673509900002108

Haldane, John. 1924. *Daedalus or Science and the Future* (New York: Dutton), https://www.gutenberg.org/files/70955/70955-h/70955-h.htm

Haraway, Donna. 2004. 'A manifesto for cyborgs: Science, technology, and social feminism in the 1980s', in *The Haraway Reader*, ed. by Donna Haraway (New York: Routledge), 7–45 (Original work published in 1985)

Haslanger, Sally. 2014. 'Social meaning and philosophical method', *Proceedings and Addresses of the American Philosophical Association* 88: 16–37

Hofmann, Bjørn. 2002. 'Is there a technological imperative in health care?', *International Journal of Technology Assessment in Health Care*, 18(3): 675–89, https://doi.org/10.1017/S0266462302000491

Horn, Claire. 2020. 'The history of the incubator makes a sideshow of mothering', *PSYCHE*, https://psyche.co/ideas/the-history-of-the-incubator-makes-a-sideshow-of-mothering

Hooton, Victoria, and Romanis, Elizabeth C. 2022. 'Artificial womb technology, pregnancy, and EU employment rights', *Journal of Law and the Biosciences*, 9(1), lsac009, https://doi.org/10.1093/jlb/lsac009

Ji, Eun-Kyung, Dolores Pretorius, Ruth Newton, K. Uyan, Andrew D. Hull, Kathryn Hollenbach, and Thomas R. Nelson. 2005. 'Effects of ultrasound on maternal-fetal bonding: A comparison of two-and three-dimensional imaging', *Ultrasound in Obstetrics and Gynecology: The Official Journal of the International Society of Ultrasound in Obstetrics and Gynecology*, 25(5): 473–77, https://doi.org/10.1002/uog.1896

Kingma, Elselijn. 2019. 'Were you a part of your mother?', *Mind*, 128(511): 609–46, https://doi.org/10.1093/mind/fzy087

Kingma, Elselijn, and Suki Finn. 2020. 'Neonatal incubator or artificial womb? Distinguishing ectogestation and ectogenesis using the metaphysics of pregnancy', *Bioethics*, 34(4): 354–63, https://doi.org/10.1111/bioe.12717

Koenig, Barbara. 1988. 'The technological imperative in medical practice: The social creation of a "routine" treatment', in *Biomedicine Examined*, ed. by Margaret Lock and Deborah Gordon (Dordrecht: Springer), 465–96, https://doi.org/10.1007/978-94-009-2725-4_18

Landau, Ruth. 2007. 'Artificial womb versus natural birth: An exploratory study of women's views', *Journal of Reproductive and Infant Psychology*, 25(1), 4–17, https://doi.org/10.1080/02646830601117118

Leifer, Myra. 1980. *Psychological Effects of Motherhood: A Study of First Pregnancy* (New York: Praeger)

Lincetto, Omella, and Banerjee, Anshu 2020. 'World prematurity day: Improving survival and quality of life for millions of babies born preterm around the world', *American Journal of Physiology-Lung Cellular and Molecular Physiology*, 319(5), L871-L874, https://doi.org/10.1152/ajplung.00479.2020

Lubetzky, Ofra. 2020. 'The maternal-fetus relationship in the uterus: Essential for wellbeing through life', *Journal of Prenatal & Perinatal Psychology & Health*, 34(6)

McCully, Sophia. 2021. 'The time has come to extend the 14-day limit', *Journal of Medical Ethics*, 47(12): e66, https://doi.org/10.1136/medethics-2020-106406

Mills, Catherine. 2014. 'Making fetal persons: Fetal homicide, ultrasound, and the normative significance of birth', *Philosophia*, 4(1): 88–107, https://doi.org/10.26180/5f3f817b0a0c5

Myers II, B. E. 2014. '"Drapetomania" Rebellion, defiance and free Black insanity', in the *Antebellum United States* (Los Angeles: University of California)

Nisha, Zairu. 2021. 'Technicization of "birth" and "mothering": Bioethical debates from feminist perspectives', *Asian Bioethics Review*, 13, 133–48, https://doi.org/10.1007/s41649-021-00169-z

Partridge, Emily, Marcus Davey, Matthew Hornick, Patrick McGovern, Ali Mejaddam, Jesse Vrecenak, Carmen Mesas-Burgos, Aliza Olive, Robert Caskey, Theodore Weiland, Jiancheng Han, Alexander Schupper, James Connelly, Kevin Dysart, Jack Rychik, Holly Hedrick, William Peranteau, and Alan Flake. 2017. 'An extra-uterine system to physiologically support the extreme premature lamb', *Nature Communications*, 8(1): 15112, https://doi.org/10.1038/ncomms15112

Perrot, Adeline, and Ruth Horn. 2022. 'The ethical landscape (s) of non-invasive prenatal testing in England, France and Germany: Findings from a comparative literature review', *European Journal of Human Genetics*, 30(6): 676–81, https://doi.org/10.1038/s41431-021-00970-2

Phillips, Bianca, and Beng Beng Ong. 2018. '"Was the infant born alive?" A review of postmortem techniques used to determine live birth in cases of suspected neonaticide', *Academic Forensic Pathology*, 8(4): 874–93, https://doi.org/10.1177/1925362118821476

Puzio, Anna. 2022. *Über-Menschen. Philosophische Auseinandersetzung mit der Anthropologie des Transhumanismus* (Bielefeld: transcript Verlag), https://doi.org/10.14361/9783839463055

Rifkin, Jeremy. 2002. 'The end of pregnancy', *The Guardian*, https://www.theguardian.com/world/2002/jan/17/gender.medicalscience

Rohwer, Yasha, and Emma Marris. 2018. 'An analysis of potential ethical justifications for mammoth de-extinction and a call for empirical research', *Ethics, Policy & Environment*, 21(1): 127–42, https://doi.org/10.1080/21550085.2018.1448043

Romanis, Elizabeth C. 2018. 'Artificial womb technology and the frontiers of human reproduction: Conceptual differences and potential implications', *Journal of Medical Ethics*, 44(11): 751–55, https://doi.org/10.1136/medethics-2018-104910

Romanis, Elizabeth. 2019. 'Artificial womb technology and the significance of birth: Why gestatelings are not newborns (or fetuses)', *Journal of Medical Ethics*, 45(11): 728–31, http://doi.org/10.1136/medethics-2019-105495

Romanis, Elizabeth, Dunja Begović, Margot Brazier, and Alexandra Katherine Mullock. 2020. 'Reviewing the womb', *Journal of Medical Ethics*, 47(12): 820–29, https://doi.org/10.1136/medethics-2020-106160

Rothman, Barbara Katz. 1991. *In Labor: Women and Power in the Birthplace.* (New York: W. W. Norton & Co)

Rothman, David. 1997. *Beginnings Count: The Technological Imperative in American Health Care* (New York; Oxford: Oxford University Press)

Ruf, Simon. 2001. 'Über-Menschen. Elemente einer genealogie des cyborgs', in *Mediale Anatomien. Menschenbilder als Medienprojektionen (Kultur- und Medientheorie)*, ed. by Annette Keck and Nicolas Pethes (Bielefeld: transcript), 267–86, https://doi.org/10.14361/9783839400760-015

Ruspini, Elisabetta. 2015. *Diversity in Family Life: Gender, Relationships and Social Change* (Bristol: Policy Press)

Schwartz, Oscar. 2019. 'On the history of the artificial womb', *JSTOR Daily*, https://daily.jstor.org/on-the-history-of-the-artificial-womb/

Singer, Peter, and Deaene Wells. 2006. 'Ectogenesis', in *Ectogenesis*, ed. by Scott Gelfand and John Shook (Amsterdam; New York: Rodopi), 9–25, https://doi.org/10.1163/9789401203456_005

Sullivan, Lawrence, and Nancy Liu-Sullivan. 2021. *Historical Dictionary of Chinese Culture* (London: Rowman & Littlefield Publishers)

Thweatt, Jeanine. 2016. *Cyborg Selves. A Theological Anthropology of the Posthuman* (London: Routledge), https://doi.org/10.4324/9781315575728

——. 2018. 'Cyborg-Christus: Transhumanismus und die Heiligkeit des Körpers', in *Designobjekt Mensch. Die Agenda des Transhumanismus auf dem Prüfstand*, ed. by Benedikt Göcke and Frank Meier-Hamidi (Freiburg: Herder), 363–76

Tong-Hyun, Kim. (2023 29 June). "South Koreans grow younger overnight as the country changes how it counts people's ages." https://apnews.com/article/south-korea-age-counting-law-a38a4a6b47c6864bd13433fdac071cec

Tronto, Joan. 1993. *Moral Boundaries: A Political Argument for an Ethics of Care* (New York; London: Routledge)

Usuda, Haruo, Shimpei Watanabe, Masatoshi Saito, Shinichi Sato, Gabrielle C. Musk, Erin Fee, Sean Carter, Yusaku Kumagai, Tsukasa Takahashi, Shinichi Kawamura, Takushi Hanita, Shigeo Kure, Nobuo Yaegashi, John P. Newnham, and Matthew W. Kemp. 2019. 'Successful use of an artificial placenta to support extremely preterm ovine fetuses at the border of viability', *American Journal of Obstetrics and Gynecology*, 221(1): 69.e1–69.e17. https://doi.org/10.1016/j.ajog.2019.03.001

Van der Hout-van der Jagt, Beatrijs, Joanne Verweij, Peter Andriessen, Willem de Boode, Arend Bos, Frank Delbressine, Alex Eggink, Jan Jaap Erwich, Loe Feijs, Floris Groenendaal, Boris Kramer, Titia Lely Rachel Loop, Franziska Neukamp, Wes Onland, Martijn Oudijk, Arjan te Pas, Irwin Reiss, Mark Schoberer, Ralph Scholten, Marc Spaanderman, Myrthe van der Ven, Marijn Vermeulen, Frans van de Vosse, and Guid Oei. 2022. 'Interprofessional consensus regarding design requirements for liquid-based Perinatal Life Support (PLS) technology', *Frontiers in Pediatrics*, 9: 1601, https://doi.org/10.3389/fped.2021.793531

Verbeek, Peter-Paul. 2008. 'Obstetric ultrasound and the technological mediation of morality: A postphenomenological analysis', *Human Studies*, 31(1): 11–26, https://doi.org/10.1007/s10746-007-9079-0

———. 2009. 'The moral relevance of technological artifacts', in *Evaluating New Technologies* (Dordrecht: Springer), 63–77, https://doi.org/10.1007/978-90-481-2229-5_6

Verweij, Joanne, Lien De Proost, Judith van Laar, Lily Frank, Sylvia Obermann-Borstn, Marijn Vermeulen, Sophie van Baalen, Beatrijs van der Hout-van der Jagt, and Elselijn Kingma. 2021. 'Ethical development of artificial amniotic sac and placenta technology: A roadmap', *Frontiers in Pediatrics*, 9: 793308, https://doi.org/10.3389/fped.2021.793308

Vollmer, Brigitte, and Caroline Edmonds. 2019. 'School age neurological and cognitive outcomes of fetal growth retardation or small for gestational age birth weight', *Frontiers in Endocrinology*, 10: 186, https://doi.org/10.3389/fendo.2019.00186

6. Conceptual Disruption and the Ethics of Technology

Lead author: Jeroen Hopster[1]
Contributing authors: *Philip Brey, Michael Klenk,*
Guido Löhr, Samuela Marchiori, Björn Lundgren,
Kevin Scharp

This chapter provides a theoretical lens on conceptual disruption. It offers a typology of conceptual disruption, discusses its relation to conceptual engineering, and sketches a programmatic view of the implications of conceptual disruption for the ethics of technology. We begin by distinguishing between three different types of conceptual disruptions: conceptual gaps, conceptual overlaps, and conceptual misalignments. Subsequently, we distinguish between different mechanisms of conceptual disruption and two modes of conceptual change. We point out that disruptions may be induced by technology but can also be triggered by intercultural exchanges. Conceptual disruptions frequently yield conceptual uncertainty and may call for conceptual and ethical inquiry. We argue that a useful approach to addressing conceptual disruptions is to engage in conceptual engineering. We outline what conceptual engineering involves and argue that discussions on conceptual disruption and conceptual engineering can benefit

---

1   All mentioned authors contributed in some way to this chapter and approved the final version. JH is the lead author of this chapter. He coordinated the contributions to this chapter, outlined its structure, and did the final editing. SM wrote a first version of Section 6.1. GL wrote a first version of Section 6.2 and Section 6.3. KS wrote a first version of Section 6.4. PB wrote a first version of Section 6.5. MK and BL commented on the chapter and modified it.

from closer integration. In closing, we discuss the relevance of studying conceptual disruption for the field of technology ethics, and point to the promise of this line of research to innovate practical philosophy at large.

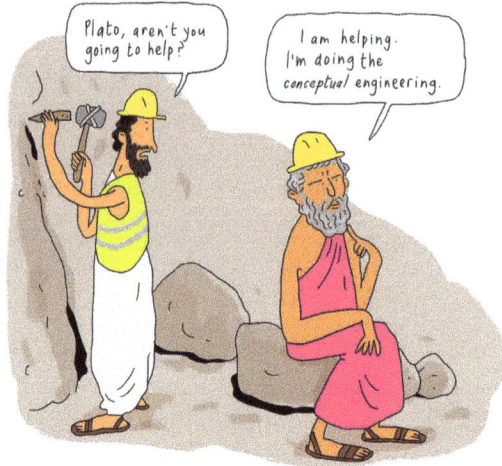

Fig. 6.1 Conceptual engineering. Credit: Menah Wellen

6.1 Introduction

The aim of this final chapter is to provide a theoretical lens on a core theme of the preceding chapters: conceptual disruption and the need for conceptual change. What kinds of conceptual disruptions can be distinguished? How can philosophers and ethicists address them? And what is the relevance of studying conceptual disruption for ethical theory and for practical philosophy at large? We start by recounting some of the conceptual disruptions that have been discussed in the previous chapters and offer further leads to theorize about them. Next, we point to some of the different causal triggers of conceptual disruption, which include not only technologies, but also intercultural dialogue. Thereafter, we introduce a recent philosophical approach that can help in addressing conceptual disruptions: conceptual engineering. We conclude by discussing the relevance of conceptual disruption for technology ethics and by stating its promise as a future research program that can benefit practical philosophy at large.

Before we get into the topic of this chapter, we should emphasize that conceptual disruption is not the only aspect of socially disruptive technologies worthy of ethicists' attention. So are 'social disruptions' more generally. Many of the examples that have been discussed throughout the previous chapters concern 'social disruptions' (Hopster, 2021a), i.e. social dynamics, often fostered by emerging technologies, whereby important aspects of human society are prevented from continuing as before, provoking normative disorientation, and giving rise to a variety of ethical and social challenges. Social disruptions may also involve the disruption of concepts, but social disruptions are not limited to conceptual disruptions. Social change occurs at many levels, and the conceptual level may not always be the most salient or interesting one.[2]

Yet, one reason for focusing specifically on conceptual disruption in this chapter is that, up until recently, this has been a relatively neglected topic of inquiry in the ethics of technology, and more so than the topic of social disruption. It is an explicit ambition of the ESDiT program to put conceptual disruption on the map of academic scholarship, and this concluding chapter provides several leads to develop that ambition. But in stating this emphasis, we do not wish to downplay the importance of social disruption as a distinct and relevant topic of ethical inquiry. Spelling out the precise nature of social disruptions, as well as its ethical implications (e.g. Hopster, 2021b; O'Neill, 2022), remains a core focus within ESDiT. This chapter simply has a different focus.

6.2 Types of conceptual disruptions

In the introduction, we defined conceptual disruption as a challenge to the meaning of a concept that prompts a possible future revision of it. This challenge may pertain to individual concepts, and also to our

---

2   Moreover, not all conceptual disruptions are entangled with social disruptions. There can be instances where concepts are challenged, but where this challenge does not emerge from societal disruptions (e.g. the introduction of the Archeae as an independent biological kingdom could be regarded as a significant conceptual disruption, but with no societal implications). Social and conceptual disruption are related, but distinct.

conceptual scheme as a whole. We argued that conceptual disruptions can be interpreted in three ways, and that technology typically plays a prominent role in each of them (Hopster and Löhr, 2023). First, we may be faced with a 'conceptual gap'. That is, we lack the concepts needed to describe a novel technological artifact, or to normatively evaluate the new impacts and affordances to which it gives rise. Second, we may be faced with a 'conceptual overlap'. That is, more than one of our existing concepts may be appropriate to describe and evaluate a novel technology, but there is uncertainty as to which concept is most suitable. Third, there may be cases of 'conceptual misalignment'. In such cases, existing concepts *do* seem applicable to conceptualize a new technology and its impacts and affordances. However, this apparent good fit actually masks an underlying value misalignment: the concept and its use do not express the values that a community of concept-users, upon ethical reflection, would like it to express.

When thinking about conceptual disruption in these terms, one should be sensitive to various problems that lurk in the background. First, for any given example, the most appropriate framing may itself be contested: what may be regarded as a conceptual gap by some ('the problem is that we lack an appropriate concept of X!'), may be understood as an overlap by others ('no, the real problem is that we have conflicting concepts of X!'). Second, talk of 'conceptual disruption' may suggest a somewhat reified and monistic understanding of concepts: it may leave the impression that the meaning and extension of concepts is always clearcut, and that there is one dominant concept or conception that gets disrupted. Such an understanding might assume more conceptual agreement than actually exists and ignore a great deal of disagreement and diversity. Furthermore, one might worry that cases of conceptual overdetermination can sometimes be unproblematic and may even be fruitful: conceptual overlaps create room for a plurality of plausible interpretation that can be tailored to specific contexts or domains. We think these are legitimate concerns. Endorsing a reified and monistic understanding of conceptual disruption constitutes a pitfall that a plausible account should expressly avoid.

Yet, when keeping these pitfalls in mind, conceptual disruption can be a fruitful concept for philosophical inquiry, and it is helpfully understood in terms of gaps, overlaps, and misalignments. Can we identify instances of these three types of conceptual disruption in the examples discussed in the preceding chapters? Consider the examples of social robotics, outlined in Chapter 3. We observed that social robots are blurring the line between 'alive' and 'lifelike': we intuitively perceive social robots as being alive in some sense, although we are aware that they are not (Carpinella et al., 2017; Spatola and Chaminade, 2022). This could be interpreted in terms of a conceptual overlap: both sides of dichotomous concepts like 'alive' and 'lifeless', or 'animate' and 'inanimate', seem applicable to social robots. At the same time, progress in social robotics arguably gives rise to conceptual gaps. Consider the binary distinction between 'moral agency' and 'moral patiency'. Arguably, there is reason to ascribe some positive moral status to intelligent machines. But neither paradigm examples of entities having moral agent-status (reflective humans), nor examples of entities having moral patient-status (sentient animals), provide a solid model for such ascriptions. Perhaps we need to articulate different notions of moral status such as the 'relational status' advocated by Gunkel (2018) and Coeckelbergh (2010), or distinguish between different gradations of moral status. Differently put: arguably the emergence of social robots points to a conceptual gap which calls for making changes to our existing conceptual framework, with regard to a cluster of important moral concepts (moral status; moral agency; moral patiency; associated notions of responsibility; *etc*).[3]

The third type of conceptual disruption we identified are conceptual misalignments. Does social robotics also give rise to this type of conceptual disruption? Recall that social robots often take on a humanlike form, which may come with certain advantages, but also engenders certain risks. Authors who emphasize the downsides of humanoid robots have argued, for instance, that anthropomorphizing robots encourages unwanted disruptions to our moral system, which, in turn, 'could seriously disrupt our ability to govern, as well as our economy' (Bryson, 2018: 22). One way to interpret this worry is in terms

---

3   This example could also be understood as a case of 'moral disruption' (Baker, 2013; Nickel, 2020; Rueda et al., 2022), since the concepts at issue — moral agency and patiency — are quintessential concepts of moral theorizing. To the extent that conceptual disruptions call for rethinking these foundational moral concepts, or their precise extension, conceptual disruptions have direct implications for ethical theory and moral practice, and conceptual disruptions are entangled with moral disruptions.

of conceptual misalignment. If we were to extend our concept of moral patiency to social robots, Bryson worries, then we are conceptualizing a novel technology using a concept that *prima facie* appears to have a good fit, but that upon reflection actually involves a misfit with other concepts and values. Our concept of 'moral patient' may be naturally extended to robots, but on further consideration, the moral implications of doing so are contentious. Assuming this view, then, we should conceptualize novel technologies in such a way that conceptual misalignments do not transpire.

We discussed another example of conceptual misalignment in chapter two, when considering the relation between the concepts of 'demos', 'democracy', and 'public sphere'. By giving citizens and non-citizens equal substantive access to online political debates that shape the political agenda, social media has severed the conceptual relationship between the 'demos' and 'public sphere', giving rise to a conceptual misalignment. Note that such a misalignment may only become apparent upon ethical reflection. This is what sets conceptual misalignments apart from conceptual gaps and overlaps: in the case of misalignment, our conceptual scheme continues to function fluently, yet in a way that is ethically problematic, as the functioning does not reflect how concepts *should* be aligned.

Conceptual gaps, overlaps and misalignments are useful terms for studying conceptual disruption. But not all the case studies discussed in this book straightforwardly adhere to this tripartite distinction. As noted, conceptual changes are not always disruptive, in the sense that they do not always overturn a well-articulated conceptual status quo. Conceptual changes can also (and often do) occur in contexts of uncertainty, where norms of conceptual application are contested, or vague. Robots challenge our understanding of the human, but what the concept of 'a human' and 'human nature' (Hannon and Lewens, 2018) amounts to has itself been contested throughout intellectual history. These are 'essentially contested concepts' (Gallie, 1955), which are continuously being disputed when it comes to their interpretation. Novel technologies can give powerful impetus to rethinking and conceptualizing them anew, but in doing so they do not always disrupt a clearly established conceptual status quo. Consider the distinction between what is internal and external to the human body, which is challenged and blurred by various technological artifacts, such as ventricular assists, or the artificial womb (Chapter 5). Arguably, the boundary between what is external and internal to the body (and the associated social and moral norms) was never clearly established. New disruptive technologies, however, prompt us to clarify this distinction, such that new norms can be established (e.g. is shutting off an artificial womb by a third party a violation of bodily integrity?). Here, conceptual disruption involves a call for clarification and conceptual articulation, where conceptual frameworks were previously vague or indeterminate.

We noted that conceptual specification should not always be regarded as a *desideratum*. The ambiguity and indeterminacy of conceptual frameworks may serve some functions, for instance as it allows for flexibility and context-specificity. Yet there are conditions in which the articulation of clear conceptual norms is called for. Consider the challenges of ascribing responsibility in the context of climate change (Chapter 4). For global geo-engineering technologies, we observed that ascribing responsibility is a very daunting task. Yet at the same time, articulating applicable notions of responsibility also seems of the utmost importance, given the major significance of the challenge at hand and the need to adequately respond to it (e.g. Jamieson, 2015). According to some, we need an adequate concept of responsibility to maintain a moral community; according to others, we need the concept of responsibility to uphold moral agency, or to help to steer actions in a desirable way.

Revising the concept of 'responsibility' in the face of new technological pressures might initially appear to be an isolated conceptual change. But as many of the examples we have discussed in this book showcase, conceptual disruptions are typically not limited to single concepts. Instead, they challenge clusters of interrelated concepts (Löhr, 2023). Consider the conceptual disruptions brought about by reproductive technologies as introduced in Chapter 5, which challenge our concepts of 'mother', 'father', and 'parent', as well as our concepts of 'birth', 'beginning of life', and 'personhood'. Similarly, social media challenge our concepts of 'demos', 'democratic public sphere', and 'self-rule' (Cf. Section 2.3), social robots challenge our concepts of 'agency' and 'moral patiency' (Cf. Section 1.4 and Section 3.3). The same holds for climate engineering technologies: these do not only challenge our concept of 'responsibility', but also the associated notions of 'agency' and 'control' (Cf. Section 4.3).

Conceptual disruptions may give rise to conceptual changes, but this need not always be the case (Löhr, 2022). In fact, technological pressures may also give impetus to conceptual preservation (Lindauer, 2020). Consider once again the concept of 'democratic public sphere', addressed in Chapter 2. The advent of social media appears to have called into question the necessity and usefulness of referring to geopolitical factors to identify the democratic public sphere. In doing so, it has made it arduous to pinpoint exactly *where* such a public sphere exists. However, this conceptual disruption has not challenged the concept of 'democratic public sphere' as such. Instead, it has opened the door to multiple possible conceptions of such a democratic public sphere. As such, one may argue that the concept of 'democratic public sphere' would seem to be ultimately adequate and should be preserved.

When referring to conceptual disruption, it is important to bear in mind this distinction between concepts and conceptions. Rawls (1999) famously stated that the concept of 'justice' allows for various conceptions, i.e., specific interpretations of the concept, such as his own 'justice as fairness'. Accordingly, conceptions may be understood as different interpretations that give precision to a concept, which are often contested or in some sense indeterminate (cf., Veluwenkamp et al., 2022). Some of the cases of conceptual disruption we have discussed in this book are similarly best understood as cases where new conceptions are advanced and discussed.

Frequently, however, conceptual disruptions do call for changing *concepts*, or enriching our conceptual schemes. Building on the discussion of Chapter 5, one might think that once a pregnancy can occur in an artificial womb, we also need another notion for the removal of the foetus after forty weeks of development from the artificial womb. We currently call this 'giving birth', but this concept does not seem entirely appropriate — for one, it involves two living beings, whereas the removal of a baby from the artificial womb involves only one. It may benefit us to introduce a distinct concept for this type of 'event'.

We submit, as an interim conclusion, that the study of conceptual disruption will benefit from clear criteria as to what counts as a conceptual disruption. Building on the previous discussion, we propose that the presence of a conceptual gap, overlap or misalignment can be taken as indicative of conceptual disruption. Challenges to specific *conceptions* may also qualify as conceptual disruptions, though it should be kept in mind that this is not the same as the disruption of *concepts*. We grant that, even when these criteria are further fleshed out, there might still be disagreement as to whether they apply in any particular case.

6.3 Mechanisms of conceptual disruption and modes of conceptual change

In the introduction we noted that disruptions involve both a 'disruptor', i.e. the disruption instigator, as well as an object of disruption. In this section we focus on the disruptors, i.e. the causal mechanisms of conceptual disruption. What are triggers of conceptual disruption and change?

As we have argued throughout this book, technology often constitutes such a disruptor, for instance when the introduction of technological artifacts provokes new norms or re-classifications. One should keep in mind, however, that 'technology' consists of more than artifacts alone. Technological artifacts are often embedded in more encompassing sociotechnical systems. Consequently, while technology frequently plays a substantial causal role in triggering disruptions, the arrow of causality may be difficult to discern. Consider the global climate engineering technologies discussed in Chapter 4 and the associated conceptual and social disruptions of the Anthropocene. In this case, what is the cause of disruption? Many of the key technologies at issue here — such as Solar Radiation Management — have not (yet) materialized. Yet at the same time, these technologies are entangled with visions about human control over the Earth's climate system.

Furthermore, not all conceptual disruptions are caused by technologies. Indeed, there is a variety of other causal mechanisms that can do so. Here we highlight one such mechanism, which is particularly potent as a trigger of conceptual disruption: intercultural dialogues and interactions. Consider the Ubuntu framework, mentioned in Chapter 4. Ubuntu has a notion of community that is much broader than traditional Western conceptualizations. This notion allows the inclusion of ancestors as well as future generations in the moral community (Kelbessa, 2015).

As Wiredu (1994), quoted in Chapter 4, remarks: '[I]n this moral scheme the rights of the unborn play such a cardinal role that any traditional African would be nonplussed by the debate in Western philosophy as to the existence of such rights'. Now, once Western philosophy comes into contact with this very different ontological point of view, and once Ubuntu philosophy comes into contact with the very different starting point in the West, their respective conceptual frameworks are challenged and require rethinking. This is an example of a conceptual disruption that might occur through intercultural dialogue or confrontation. Such exchanges can provide inspiration for conceptual amelioration: they broaden the horizon of conceptual possibility and allow for criticism of possible shortcomings of conceptual frameworks that are taken for granted.

Conceptual disruptions are relative to the conceptual framework that is being disrupted — and here, too, intercultural differences are highly relevant. Cultural contexts affect whether technologies are socially and conceptually disruptive. We noted that robotics technologies can disrupt the distinction between what is animate and inanimate, but in a community which endorses animist beliefs and ascribes agency to artifacts to begin with, this would not constitute much of a conceptual disruption. Or consider proposals to grant legal rights to natural entities such as forests or rivers, which disrupts traditional Western conceptions of legal personhood. Yet it does not seem very disruptive relative to the conceptual scheme of the Māori people, which is much more sensitive to the importance of protecting socio-environmental relationships (the Māori concept of rāhui, for instance, places temporary constraints on human activities to ensure immediate responses to threats of serious harms) (Watene, 2022). Hence, conceptual disruptions are relative to conceptual frameworks, which may in turn be culturally relative.

In closing this section, let us point out that apart from different mechanisms of conceptual disruption, we might also distinguish between different modes of *conceptual change*. Attempts to overcome a conceptual disruption (e.g. through conceptual engineering; see Section 6.4) may lead to conceptual change. This can happen, for instance, when technology produces novel entities (new artifacts and new consequences of the use of technology) that do not make a good fit with our conceptual scheme, so much so that adaptations seem in order. These can be superficial changes, such as the introduction of new concepts to designate the new technology and some of its uses, components and consequences. But they can also be more profound changes, which challenge fundamental philosophical concepts, like those of agency, organism, or mind. This happens, for instance, when a new technology produces hybrids that do not seem to fit existing fundamental concepts, such as intelligent robots, synthetic organisms, and brain-computer interfaces. These are conceptual changes that occur in a 'loud way', prompted by a conceptual disruption.

However, conceptual changes need not always be prompted by conceptual disruptions. We might call such an instance of conceptual change that occurs without conceptual disruption 'silent conceptual change'. One way in which such silent change can happen is when a technology generates new application domains for concepts. For example, many moral and philosophical concepts are currently reapplied in a digital context, leading to concepts such as 'digital well-being', 'digital democracy' and 'cybersecurity'. Similarly, the rise of genetic technologies now enables concepts like 'genetic privacy' and 'genetic equality'. These new technological manifestations may extend or change the meaning of the original concept. But this does not give rise to conceptual gaps, overlaps, or misalignments, at least not obviously so.

6.4 Conceptual engineering

What can we do in response to different types of conceptual disruptions? One general approach, which has attracted lots of attention in recent philosophy, seems particularly relevant for the task at hand: conceptual engineering (Scharp, 2013; Eklund, 2015; Cappelen, 2018; Burgess and Plunkett, 2013a; 2013b; Cappelen and Plunkett, 2021).

Conceptual engineering can be understood as a branch of philosophy dedicated to investigating how best to improve our concepts and other 'representational devices'. 'Representational devices' can be understood, roughly, as more or less accurate mental images of what the world is like. The central question for conceptual engineers is whether, when, why, and how we ought to change our concepts (and other representational devices). For example, should we strive to use concepts that are as accurate as possible, that 'carve nature at its joints', so to speak? Or are there perhaps criteria other than accurate representation that should guide us in choosing the concepts we use? Thus, conceptual engineering covers questions about how to assess existing concepts, how to create new ones, and how to implement new conceptual proposals in actual populations of concept-users. Philosophers who work in the field of conceptual engineering are also interested in the *ethics* of changing our conceptual repertoires. In short, the field covers the philosophically relevant issues in the process of intentionally changing the concepts we use to think, or the meanings we use to communicate.

Conceptual engineering is frequently contrasted with conceptual analysis: rather than unveiling the meaning of our concepts, the aim of the former is to *change* concepts, on the basis of moral, epistemic, or other considerations. Thus, *conceptual engineering* is strongly associated (and sometimes identified) with *conceptual ethics* — the study of which concepts we should choose — rather than the study of which concepts we have already chosen in our public language. Conceptual engineering, then, is a way of intentionally engineering or changing our conceptual repertoire.

Although intentionally changing concepts has been a prominent feature of Western philosophy and science for centuries, it has recently become a major area of philosophical inquiry itself (e.g. Haslanger, 2000; Scharp, 2013; Burgess et al., 2020; Cappellen, 2018). That is, conceptual engineering is an approach to doing philosophy as much as it is an area of philosophical inquiry. There are prominent debates in the history of philosophy that are clearly about conceptual engineering, such as the debate between Carnap and Strawson about the method of explication, which we discuss below. However, the field as a whole is relatively young, with major works published only in the early 2000s.

Conceptual engineering can be undertaken for many different reasons and in different ways. Chalmers (2020) distinguishes between *de novo engineering* and *re-engineering*: de novo engineering consists of the construction of new concepts, whereas re-engineering is 'fixing' or 'replacing' existing concepts. More broadly, one might distinguish between three ways of engineering our conceptual schemes: (i) changing an existing concept in a way that retains that very concept through the change; (ii) replacing an existing concept with a new one that is intended to perform better than the old one; (iii) introducing a totally new concept that has no ancestors. Each of these kinds of projects brings unique desiderata and success conditions. It is crucial to keep these distinctions in mind when characterizing or evaluating a given conceptual engineering proposal.

For purposes of this book, we are particularly interested in projects of conceptual engineering that arise in response to technological disruptions. Not all projects of conceptual engineering fit these parameters. Indeed, the 'engineering' metaphor notwithstanding, until recently, mainstream work in conceptual engineering has not focused much on conceptual engineering in response to technological developments (Hopster and Löhr, 2023). However, as examples from the previous chapters illustrate, technology often plays a prominent role in conceptual disruption and conceptual change, in many more instances than previously noticed and discussed. Those interested in the debate about conceptual engineering are natural allies of those who investigate technological and moral change.

Consider the definition of a 'planet' by the International Astronomical Union (IAU). Prior to the late twentieth century, it was commonly believed by scientists and the public that there were a relatively small number of planets, certainly fewer than one hundred, and perhaps a large number of smaller objects orbiting the sun. With advances in astronomical technology, scientists discovered a large number of objects in the Kuiper belt that are similar in size to Pluto. Moreover, they expected to find hundreds or even thousands of these objects. The new astronomical technology led to a conceptual disruption: (i) most people believed there were a small number of planets orbiting the sun, but (ii) scientists discovered using the new technology that there are hundreds of objects like Pluto orbiting the sun. Claim (i) seems to be something like a conceptual truth about the idea of a 'planet'. Claim (ii) is the scientific discovery that came from technological advancement, leading to the conclusion that there are hundreds of planets. Scientists felt it was urgent to address this conceptual disruption. They could have embraced the claim that there are hundreds of planets in our solar system. This option, however, would have required major changes in our concept of 'planet' since being a planet would no longer be a special category with only a few members. The other option was to redefine the term 'planet' so as to exclude the hundreds of Kuiper belt objects, and this is the line the IAU actually pursued.

This account of the new definition of 'planet' and the uproar about Pluto illustrates the three stages typically involved in processes of conceptual engineering. First, a conceptual challenge arises, which is often brought about by new technologies. Second, conceptual engineers question what should be done about this disruption. A key issue that arises at this second stage, with an eye to procedural justice, is the question of who is involved in arriving at this verdict. Is it a call for a certain group of experts to make, such as the IAU in the case of Pluto? Or should others be involved? The third stage is that of implementation: how do conceptual engineers go about spreading the word and ensure uptake in relevant communities of concept users?

By what standards should we decide on the aptness of our concepts? This is the question about appropriate criteria for the conceptual engineering process. One possibility, advocated by Sally Haslanger, is to connect the project of conceptual amelioration — improving our concepts — specifically with social and political aims. For example, Haslanger (2000) argues that we should drop the terms 'mother' and 'father' and only use the term 'parent', to facilitate the fight for gender equality. But the success conditions of conceptual engineering might also be understood in different terms, which need not be explicitly social or political.

The questions we are asking here, to use an analogy from the field of engineering and design, concern the appropriate 'design requirements' for engineering concepts. Related questions include the following: When ought one spend the time to evaluate a concept and decide whether it is effective enough to keep as is? When ought one investigate possible changes when one identifies a conceptual disruption? What is the best way to decide on a course of action to implement a conceptual engineering project? One kind of answer appeals to the idea that concepts have a function, and that the need for conceptual engineering arises insofar as we need to improve that function, ensure its continuation, or prevent it from failure. This perspective naturally leads to a question about the nature of conceptual functions, which is a debated issue in the current conceptual engineering literature (Queloz, 2019; Klenk, 2021). For present purposes, we need not take any stance in that particular debate; what matters is that concepts serve *some* function which we deem desirable, such that conceptual changes can potentially be regarded as adaptations or improvements — changes which make it the case that concepts better serve this function. Still other scholars wonder whether concepts have any functions that can be specified in a substantive way.

In closing this section, it is important to bear in mind that the field of conceptual engineering is not without dispute. There are various problems that critics of conceptual engineering have raised. Let us consider one such problem: the challenge that changing concepts amounts to changing the subject. On Carnap's understanding, conceptual engineering can be understood as a method of explication which advises philosophers to provide determinate, scientifically rigorous definitions for important philosophical terms that hitherto had fuzzy or merely intuitive definitions. Strawson's objection to explication has come to be seen as a basic issue that almost any conceptual engineering effort ought to be able to address (Carnap, 1950; Strawson, 1963). Strawson said essentially that explication is merely changing the subject. It does not address the original philosophical issues associated with the term in question. As such, explication ought not be seen as a legitimate philosophical methodology, because it leaves all the important philosophical problems untouched.

While there are many responses to Strawson's objection, it might be insightful to consider the planet example discussed above. This is a clear case of explication since it involved rejecting an intuitive meaning for 'planet' and adopting a more rigorous and scientifically acceptable meaning. It ought to be clear that these are two different meanings since they have two distinct extensions. Pluto is a member of the extension for the old meaning, but Pluto is not in the extension for the new meaning, and the same goes for the rest of the dwarf planets. Did the IAU merely change the subject, as an advocate of Strawson's objection would contend? They certainly did change what the word 'planet' is about. It was about a particular property and now it is about a slightly different property. So it seems like the answer is yes: the IAU did change the subject of the word 'planet', and thereby changed the subject of discussions using the word 'planet'. Was this pointless, as the Strawsonian suggests? Not at all. It is better for science to have discussions about the new subject matter, rather than about the old one. Sometimes changing the subject matter is exactly what is needed to address a problem.

6.5 Implications for ethics of technology

The aim of the ESDiT program is not just to study how fundamental and moral concepts are disrupted by emerging technologies, nor is it just to propose improved and new concepts in response. It is also to innovate ethics and political philosophy generally, and ethics and political philosophy of technology specifically. Due to social and conceptual disruptions, ethics and philosophy may not always be using an optimal conceptual framework. Improving this framework may contribute to better theories and methods in the field, which will yield better results.

This outlook rests on the view that many of the key concepts of philosophy, fundamental and moral concepts like 'nature', 'agency', 'mind', 'justice' and 'liberty' are historically contingent. They do not exist in every society and culture, and have not always existed in past epochs. Also, even when these key concepts stably exist at different times and places, their meaning often varies. This is just an historical observation, which does not entail any normative claims on whether some concepts are better than others, or whether some concepts have universal validity. But it does prompt serious inquiry into the nature of conceptual change, disruption, and modification.

This outlook also rests on the view that, as contingent constructs, concepts always have flaws and limitations and can be improved upon. Moreover, as societies change, whether these are changes in natural conditions, social and economic structures, or cultural practices and beliefs, changes in fundamental and moral concepts may be desirable so as to ensure their usefulness under new conditions. For example, with growing secularization, individualization and availability of contraceptives in the 1960s, most people have concluded that concepts like purity, chastity and temperance are no longer useful, and should be replaced by concepts more fitting to modern sexual relationships, like openness, trust, commitment and respect. Similarly, many moral and fundamental concepts of philosophy are centuries old, and may not make a great fit with our twenty-first century world. An attempt at conceptual engineering, that takes recent major changes in the world into account, would therefore be helpful.

Conceptual engineering is not new in philosophy. The field of environmental philosophy was made possible in large part because of the introduction of new concepts and changes in the meaning and scope of existing concepts. In particular, this includes the expansion of the concepts of moral patienthood and intrinsic value to include environmental entities and the introduction of the concepts of sustainability and sustainable development. Similarly, the introduction of the philosophical notion of natural equality in the seventeenth century by Hobbes and Locke, which was then translated into moral and political equality and equality before the law, has enabled the whole social contract tradition of political philosophy as well as the tradition of liberalism and its conception of individual rights. The introduction of the notion of privacy in the late nineteenth century has enabled philosophers to articulate and study a dimension of human autonomy and well-being that they might not have been able to discern and study as well otherwise.

What these examples show is that conceptual engineering, involving both the introduction of new concepts and the modification and improvement of existing ones, has historically been common in philosophy, and has helped the field to progress. We have argued in this book that unprecedented recent and forthcoming changes in society, brought about in large part by socially disruptive technologies of the recent past, present and future, require conceptual engineering of many of our fundamental philosophical and moral concepts, and that this may change our methods of doing ethics and philosophy.

Exciting challenges lie ahead. More needs to be understood about appropriate criteria and legitimate ways for conceptual engineering. That is, we should understand more about potential deficiencies that our concepts may suffer from, and legitimate goals to which they may be put to use. Insofar as the goal is to create effective change in how entire groups and societies use concepts, there is an important practical and normative question about how to implement such changes. The 'politics of implementation' (Queloz and Bieber, 2022) will be an urgent and important area for further inquiry.

Another challenge for ethics of technology is how to best study conceptual disruption and conceptual change through technology. This book has offered some building blocks for doing so, both theoretically as well through practical examples of technologies that (allegedly) disrupt existing conceptual schemes. But this leaves ample room for further refinements and raises various further questions. Consider the awareness we have raised that conceptual disruption always occurs relative to a given conceptual framework, which urges us to take a more intercultural perspective than has been common in academic philosophy. Yet how, exactly, should the conceptual schemes of a given cultural community be delineated?

Another question concerns the methods to (empirically) study conceptual disruption and change. One potential method might be the analysis of corpus linguistics. Arguably, changes in concepts, including conceptual disruption, have some correlation with changes in language and words used, for example for describing certain phenomena or asking ethical questions about them. There are various existing methods for detecting semantic change in text corpora that might also be promising for studying conceptual disruption and change (e.g. Hamilton et al., 2016). Similarly, methods are being developed to use text corpora to study value change in relation to technologies (De Wildt et al., 2022).

As we saw in the introduction, philosophy and ethics of technology do not just want to understand technologies' impacts and disruptive potential, but also seek to contribute to better technologies in a better society. They do so by closely interacting with scientists and engineers and also with policy makers. Such a contribution requires attention not just to conceptual disruption and conceptual engineering, but also to how technologies are socially disruptive in cases that do not disrupt concepts. Such a contribution may also require new methods and approaches. For example, it may require new methods for studying and developing technologies in living labs, in which their disruptive potential is both studied and addressed (e.g. through design choices) in close collaboration with designers, engineers, artists and relevant stakeholders. It may also require adaptation of existing methods for responsibly developing new technology, such as value-sensitive design (VSD) (Friedman and Hendry, 2019). For example, Veluwenkamp and

Van den Hoven (2023) have proposed an approach to integrate insights from conceptual engineering into the VSD approach.

Ultimately, addressing the challenges brought by twenty-first century technologies — such as social media, social robots, climate engineering, and the artificial womb — requires not just the engineering of technology (as traditional engineers and designers have done) or just conceptual engineering (as proposed in philosophy), but a synthetic combination of both, with an eye to the fundamental values we want to uphold.

Further listening and watching

Readers who would like to learn more about the topics discussed in this chapter might be interested in listening to these episodes of the ESDiT podcast (https://anchor.fm/esdit) and other videos:

Guido Löhr on 'Do socially disruptive technologies really change our concepts or just our conceptions?': https://podcasters.spotify.com/pod/show/esdit/episodes/Guido-Lhr-on-Do-socially-disruptive-technologies-really-change-our-concepts-or-just-our-conceptions-e1uhlj2/a-a99r808

Arché *Conceptual Engineering* series on YouTube, set up by Kevin Scharp: https://www.youtube.com/c/ConceptualEngineering

References

Babushkina, Dina, and Athanasios Votsis. 2022. 'Disruption, technology and the question of (artificial) identity', *AI & Ethics*, 2: 611–22, https://doi.org/10.1007/s43681-021-00110-y

Baker, Robert. 2013. *Before Bioethics: A History of American Medical Ethics from the Colonial Period to the Bioethics Revolution* (New York: Oxford University Press)

Bryson, Joanna. 2018. 'Patiency is not a virtue: The design of intelligent systems and systems of ethics', *Ethics and Information Technology*, 20: 15–26, https://doi.org/10.1007/s10676-018-9448-6

Burgess, Alexis, Herman Cappelen, and David Plunkett (eds). 2020. *Conceptual Engineering and Conceptual Ethics* (Oxford: Oxford University Press), https://doi.org/10.1093/oso/9780198801856.003.0001

Burgess, Alexis, and David Plunkett. 2013a. 'Conceptual ethics I', *Philosophical Compass*, 8(12): 1091–1101, https://doi.org/10.1111/phc3.12086

——. 2013b. 'Conceptual ethics II', *Philosophical Compass*, 8(12): 1102–10, https://doi.org/10.1111/phc3.12085

Cappellen, Herman. 2018. *Fixing Language: An Essay on Conceptual Engineering* (Oxford: Oxford University Press)

Cappelen, Herman, and David Plunkett. 2021. 'A guided tour of conceptual engineering and conceptual ethics', in *Conceptual Engineering and Conceptual Ethics*, ed. by Alexis Burgess, Herman Cappelen, and David Plunkett (Oxford: Oxford University Press), https://doi.org/10.1093/oso/9780198801856.003.0001

Carnap, Rudolf. 1950. *Logical Foundations of Probability* (Chicago: The University of Chicago Press)

Carpinella, Colleen, Alisa Wyman, Michael Perez, and Steven Stroessner. 2017. 'The Robotic Social Attributes Scale (RoSAS): Development and validation', *HRI '17: Proceedings of the 2017 ACM/IEEE International Conference on Human-Robot Interaction*, 254–62, https://doi.org/10.1145/2909824.3020208

Chalmers. David. 2020. 'What is conceptual engineering and what should it be?', *Inquiry*, https://doi.org/10.1080/0020174X.2020.1817141

Coeckelbergh, Mark. 2010. 'Robot rights? Towards a social-relational justification of moral consideration', *Ethics and Information Technology*, 12: 209–11, https://doi.org/10.1007/s10676-010-9235-5

De Wildt, Tristan, Ibo van de Poel, and Emile Chappin. 2022. 'Tracing long-term value change in (energy) technologies: Opportunities of probabilistic topic models using large data sets', *Science, Technology, & Human Values*, 47: 429–58, https://doi.org/10.1177/01622439211054439

Eklund, Matti. 2015. 'Intuitions, conceptual engineering, and conceptual fixed points', in *The Palgrave Handbook of Philosophical Methods*, ed. by Chris Daly (London: Palgrave), 363–85, https://doi.org/10.1057/9781137344557_15

Eriksen, Cecilie (2020). *Moral Change: Dynamics, Structure, and Normativity* (Cham: Palgrave Macmillan)

Friedman, Batya, and David Hendry. 2019. *Value Sensitive Design: Shaping Technology with Moral Imagination* (Cambridge: MIT Press)

Gallie, Walter. 1955. 'Essentially contested concepts', *Proceedings of the Aristotelian society*, 56: 167–98

Gunkel, David. 2018. *Robot Rights* (Cambridge: MIT Press)

Hamilton, William, Jure Leskovec, and Dan Jurafsky. 2016. 'Diachronic word embeddings reveal statistical laws of semantic change', in *Proceedings of the 54th Annual Meeting of the Association for Computational Linguistics (Volume 1:*

Long Papers) (Berlin: Association for Computational Linguistics), 1489–501, https://doi.org/10.18653/v1/P16-1141

Haslanger, Sally. 2000. 'Gender and race: (What) are they? (What) do we want them to be?', *Noûs*, 34(1): 31–55 https://doi.org/10.1111/0029-4624.00201

Hannon, Elizabeth, and Tim Lewens (eds). 2018. *Why We Disagree About Human Nature* (Oxford: Oxford University Press)

Hopster, Jeroen. 2021a. 'What are socially disruptive technologies?', *Technology in Society*, 67: 101750, https://doi.org/10.1016/j.techsoc.2021.101750

——. 2021b. 'The ethics of disruptive technologies: Towards a general framework', in *Advances in Intelligent Systems and Computing*, ed. by Juan de Paz Santana, Daniel de la Iglesia and Alfonso José López Rivero (Cham: Springer), https://doi.org/10.1007/978-3-030-87687-6_14

Hopster, Jeroen, and Guido Löhr. 2023. 'Conceptual engineering and philosophy of technology: Amelioration or adaptation?', Unpublished manuscript

Jacobs, Naomi (2023). 'De kunstmatige baarmoeder', *Wijsgerig Perspectief*, 1.

Jamieson, Dale. 2015. 'Responsibility and climate change', *Global Justice: Theory, Practice, Rhetoric*, 8(2): 23–47, https://doi.org/10.21248/gjn.8.2.86

Kelbessa, Workineh. 2015. 'African environmental ethics, Indigenous knowledge, and environmental challenges', *Environmental Ethics*, 37(4): 387–410, https://doi.org/10.5840/enviroethics201537439

Klenk, Michael. 2021. 'Moral realism, disagreement, and conceptual ethics', *Inquiry*, https://doi.org/10.1080/0020174X.2021.1995483

Lindauer, Matthew. 2020. 'Conceptual engineering as concept preservation', *Ratio*, 33(3): 155–62, https://doi.org/10.1111/rati.12280

Löhr, Guido. 2022. 'Linguistic interventions and the ethics of conceptual disruption', *Ethical Theory and Moral Practice*, 25: 835–49, https://doi.org/10.1007/s10677-022-10321-9

——. 2023. 'Do socially disruptive technologies really change our concepts or just our conceptions?', *Technology in Society*, 72: 102160, https://doi.org/10.1016/j.techsoc.2022.102160

Nickel, Philip. 2020. 'Disruptive innovation and moral uncertainty', *NanoEthics*, 14(3): 259–69, https://doi.org/10.1007/s11569-020-00375-3

Nickel Philip, Olya Kudina, and Ibo van de Poel. 2022. 'Moral uncertainty in technomoral change: Bridging the explanatory gap', *Perspectives on Science*, 30(2): 260–83, https://doi.org/10.1162/posc_a_00414

O'Neill, Elizabeth. 2022. 'Contextual integrity as a general conceptual tool for evaluating technological change', *Philosophy & Technology*, 35: 79, https://doi.org/10.1007/s13347-022-00574-8

Queloz, Matthieu. 2019. 'The points of concepts: Their types, tensions, and connections', *Canadian Journal of Philosophy*, 49(8): 1122–45, https://doi.org /10.1080/00455091.2019.1584940

Queloz, Matthieu, and Friedemann Bieber. 2022. 'Conceptual engineering and the politics of implementation', *Pacific Philosophical Quarterly*, 103: 670–91, https://doi.org/10.1111/papq.12394

Rawls, John. 1999. *A Theory of Justice* (Cambridge: Belknap Press)

Rueda, Jon, Jonathan Pugh, and Julian Savulescu. 2022. 'The morally disruptive future of reprogenetic enhancement technologies', *Trends in Biotechnology*, 2258: 1–4, https://doi.org/10.1016/j.tibtech.2022.10.007

Scharp, Kevin. 2013. *Replacing Truth* (Oxford: Oxford University Press)

Spatola, Nicolas, and Thierry Chaminade. 2022. 'Cognitive load increases anthropomorphism of humanoid robots. The automatic path of anthropomorphism', *International Journal of Human-Computer Studies*, 167: 102884, https://doi.org/10.1016/j.ijhcs.2022.102884

Strawson, Peter. 1963. 'Carnap's views on constructed systems versus natural languages in analytic philosophy', in *The Philosophy of Rudolf Carnap*, ed. by Paul Schilpp (LaSalle: Open Court), 503–18

Veluwenkamp, Herman, Marianna Capasso, Jonne Maas, and Lavinia Marin. 2022. 'Technology as driver for morally motivated conceptual engineering', *Philosophy & Technology*, 35: 71, https://doi.org/10.1007/s13347-022-00565-9

Veluwenkamp, Herman, and Jeroen van den Hoven. 2023. 'Design for values and conceptual engineering', *Ethics and Information Technology*, 25: 2, https:// doi.org/10.1007/s10676-022-09675-6

Watene, K. 2022. 'Indigenous philosophy and intergenerational justice', in *Reimagining the Human-Environment Relationship*. United Nations University, http://collections.unu.edu/eserv/UNU:8829/UNUUNEP_Watene_RHER. pdf

Wiredu, Kwasi. 1994. 'Philosophy, humankind and the environment', in *Philosophy, Humanity, and Ecology*, ed. by H. Odera Oruka (Nairobi: ACTS Press)

Glossary

Anthropocene: i.e. 'the epoch of humankind', describes how technology-driven human activities such as the burning of fossil fuels have propelled the earth into a new geological epoch distinct from the previous Holocene epoch

Anthropomorphism: attributing human characteristics to non-human entities such as robots

Artificial intelligence: technologies that are able to perform or take over tasks that human beings use their natural intelligence to perform

Artificial womb (or ectogestative device): a device that enables the extra-uterine gestation of a human being, or mammal more generally

Bioenergy with Carbon Capture and Storage (BECCS): burning biomass that absorbs carbon dioxide (CO_2) as it grows for energy production, with the resulting emissions captured and stored underground or in chemically stable ways such as in minerals

Carbon Dioxide Removal techniques (CDR): also known as 'Negative emissions techniques', these techniques remove carbon dioxide (CO_2) from the atmosphere and store it in various forms. CDR is one of the two main categories of climate engineering

Climate engineering: deliberate and large-scale intervention in the Earth's climate system in order to moderate global warming

Conceptual change: changes of a concept or conceptual scheme that occur over time

Conceptual disruption: a challenge to the meaning of a concept or cluster of concepts, which may prompt a future revision

Conceptual engineering: an approach to doing philosophy, as well as an area of philosophical inquiry, dedicated to investigating how best to improve our concepts

Conceptual gap: a hiatus in our conceptual scheme, often triggered by new technological artifacts, actions, or relations

Conceptual misalignment: a lack of alignment between a given concept and other concepts and values, due to conceptual change

Conceptual overlap: a situation in which there is more than one concept that fits to describe a new type of artifact, action or event

Democracy: system of political representation based on the choice of government by free and equal citizens

Demos: the governed population

Ectogestative device (or artificial womb): a device that enables the extra-uterine gestation of a human being, or mammal more generally

Full-ectogestation: complete process of extra-uterine gestation from fertilization to birth (currently not possible and also not intended by the scientists who are developing the technology)

Humanoid robot: a robot designed to look and/or behave like a human being

Interculturality: equal exchange or communication between different cultures or cultural groups

Moral agent: an entity or being that is capable of moral action and moral decision-making

Moral hazard: the availability of climate engineering could decrease the political commitment to ramp up radical mitigation.

Moral patient: an entity or being towards which moral agents can have moral duties, i.e. an entity that should be treated with moral consideration

Partial-ectogestation: extra-uterine gestation following a transfer from the maternal womb (for therapeutic purposes)

Precautionary Principle: principle that tells to refraining from action if the nature or the magnitude of certain consequences are unacceptable. In other words, lack of full scientific knowledge about a potential risk is insufficient reasons to assume that there is no risk

Robot: a machine that is equipped with sensors and actuators with the help of which it can interact with its environment in the service of specific tasks

Self-government: the ability of an individual or a population to govern themselves in a relatively autonomous manner

Social disruption: changes that prevent important aspects of human society (broadly understood) from continuing as usual, thereby generating disorder or upheaval

Social media: technical system that connects users together, allowing them to share information, communicate, and comment on posted information in real time.

Social robot: a robot designed to interact with human beings in distinctively social ways

Solar Radiation Modification (SRM): techniques to affect the planetary reflection levels and by that decrease one of the effects of climate change (i.e. warming). SRM is one of the two main categories of climate engineering

Stratospheric Aerosol Injection (SAI): injects a gas into the atmosphere which then changes into aerosols that block some incoming solar radiation, slightly lowering global average temperature.

Technomoral change: change in moral routines triggered by (new) technology

Viability: ability of a fetus to survive outside of a uterus

Index

About the Team

Alessandra Tosi was the managing editor for this book.

Elizabeth Pitts proof-read this manuscript. Lucy Barnes indexed it.

Jeevanjot Kaur Nagpal designed the cover. The cover was produced in InDesign using the Fontin font.

Laura Rodriguez Pupo distributed and marketed this book.

Jeremy Bowman typeset the book in InDesign and produced the paperback and hardback editions. The text font is Tex Gyre Pagella; the heading font is Californian FB.

Cameron Craig produced the EPUB, PDF, HTML, and XML editions — the conversion was made with open-source software such as pandoc (https://pandoc.org/), created by John MacFarlane, and other tools freely available on our GitHub page (https://github.com/ OpenBookPublishers).

This book has also been peer-reviewed anonymously by experts in their field. We thank them for their invaluable help.

This book need not end here...

Share

All our books — including the one you have just read — are free to access online so that students, researchers and members of the public who can't afford a printed edition will have access to the same ideas. This title will be accessed online by hundreds of readers each month across the globe: why not share the link so that someone you know is one of them?

This book and additional content is available at:
doi.org/10.11647/OBP.0366

Donate

Open Book Publishers is an award-winning, scholar-led, not-for-profit press making knowledge freely available one book at a time. We don't charge authors to publish with us: instead, our work is supported by our library members and by donations from people who believe that research shouldn't be locked behind paywalls.

Why not join them in freeing knowledge by supporting us:
https://www.openbookpublishers.com/support-us

Follow @OpenBookPublish 🐦

Read more at the Open Book Publishers **BLOG**

You may also be interested in:

The Era of Global Risk
An Int roduction to Existential Risk Studies
SJ Beard, Martin Rees, Catherine Richards,
Clarissa Rios Rojas (eds)
https://doi.org/10.11647/OBP.0336

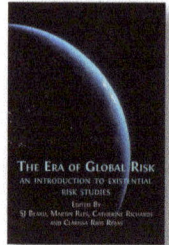

Chance Encounters
Kristien Hens
https://doi.org/10.11647/OBP.0320

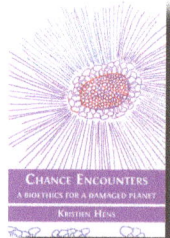

Technology, Media Literacy, and the Human Subject
A Posthuman Approach
Richard S. Lewis
https://doi.org/10.11647/OBP.0253

Human and Machine Consciousness
David Gamez
https://doi.org/10.11647/OBP.0107

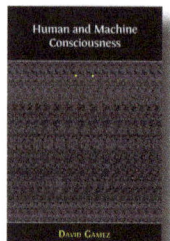

www.ingramcontent.com/pod-product-compliance
Lightning Source LLC
Chambersburg PA
CBHW040411110426
42812CB00012B/2522